A Book of House Plans
Floor Plans for Original Designs of Various Architectural Types

by W.H. Butterfield and H.W. Tuttle

with an introduction by Roger Chambers

This work contains material that was originally published in 1912.

This publication is within the Public Domain.

*This edition is reprinted for educational purposes
and in accordance with all applicable Federal Laws.*

Introduction Copyright 2017 by Roger Chambers

Self Reliance Books

Get more historic titles on animal and stock breeding, gardening and old fashioned skills by visiting us at:

http://selfreliancebooks.blogspot.com/

Introduction

I am pleased to present yet another title on Homesteading and Farm Life.

This volume is entitled "A Book of House Plans" and was published in 1912.

The work is in the Public Domain and is re-printed here in accordance with Federal Laws.

As with all reprinted books of this age that are intended to perfectly reproduce the original edition, considerable pains and effort had to be undertaken to correct fading and sometimes outright damage to existing proofs of this title. At times, this task is quite monumental, requiring an almost total "rebuilding" of some pages from digital proofs of multiple copies. Despite this, imperfections still sometimes exist in the final proof and may detract from the visual appearance of the text.

I hope you enjoy reading this book as much as I enjoyed making it available to readers again.

Roger Chambers

Fig. 11—C. E. COLBURN'S FARM AND STOCK BARN

Fig. 19—MR. LAWSON VALENTINE'S BARN, "HOUGHTON FARM," MOUNTAINVILLE, N. Y.

CONTENTS

	PAGE
A General Description of the Plans	9
Cost	18
A Vacation Home—Design No. 1	25
An English Stucco Cottage—Design No. 2	31
A Modified Dutch Colonial Type—Design No. 3	37
A Colonial House for a Village Street—Design No. 4	43
An Italian Villa—Design No. 5	49
A Stucco Bungalow—Design No. 6	55
An English Half-timber Cottage—Design No. 7	61
A Southern Colonial House—Design No. 8	67
A Spanish Mission Type—Design No. 9	73
A Stucco House for a Narrow Lot—Design No. 10	79
A House Based on the New England Colonial—Design No. 11	85
A Gabled House of Half-timber—Design No. 12	91
A Long Gambrel-roof House—Design No. 13	97
A Swiss Chalet—Design No. 14	103
A Modified Colonial Cottage—Design No. 15	109
A Small Dutch Colonial House—Design No. 16	115
An Informal English Cottage—Design No. 17	125
A Frame House of Italian Simplicity—Design No. 18	131
A Colonial House of Simple Lines—Design No. 19	137
A Combination of Stucco with Half-timber Gables—Design No. 20	143
A Stucco Cottage—Design No. 21	149

A BOOK OF HOUSE PLANS

A BOOK OF HOUSE PLANS

A GENERAL DESCRIPTION OF THE PLANS

TO design a small country house possessing artistic and economic features, the construction of which may be accomplished for a minimum amount, is not among the simplest problems of the architectural profession. The most satisfactory solutions are arrived at by a process of elimination, resulting in a compact plan possessing the essential requirements of the average home-builder, and arranged in such a manner that the total area is proportionately divided to best suit the uses for which each unit of the plan is intended.

The houses shown on the following pages have been carefully designed to meet the requirements of the average family desiring a house of moderate size and pleasing appearance. They are taken from the actual working drawings or from houses already erected. The aim of the authors has been to emphasize the really essential features and eliminate all that might be considered superfluous or not consistent in a house of moderate cost. Simplicity of plan and exterior treatment means economy but not necessarily ugliness. The success of an architectural design, in a building of any description depends principally upon its proportion, scale and fenestration, and no amount of elaboration can atone for a poorly proportioned building. Bearing all this in mind, we have planned our houses, knowing that the people who will live in them will prefer to have their rooms as large as possible for the price they pay and to have the construction and materials of the best throughout. We know that buildings cost so much per cubic foot or square foot of ground area. When we attempt to build a small or medium-sized house with extra rooms, such as libraries, reception rooms, large halls or billiard-rooms, we must do one of two things: either reduce the size of all the rooms, or count on poor workmanship and cheap materials. As the ground area is limited, these additions must necessarily occupy part of the space that should be devoted to the more important rooms. The average person certainly cares more for a house of fewer well proportioned, livable rooms, of good materials and well built, than for a house cut up into small or irregular rooms and poorly constructed.

Aside from the general proportion of the various rooms in relation to each other, another vital problem in house planning is proper circulation, which is the result of the correct position of the important rooms in relation to each other. The solution of this phase of small house planning is far more difficult than in the larger type, where passages may be introduced to bring about direct communication between various parts of the house without seeming inconsistent or extravagant.

It will be seen by examining the following plans that the problem of good circulation has been carefully considered. Aside from a few designs of an exceptional type (in every case the smaller and more compact examples), it is apparent that the living-rooms are well protected against intrusion from the service quarters, except as may be required in the performance of the usual domestic duties.

The living-room and dining-room are either intercommunicating or are connected by means of the main hall, an arrangement many people prefer, largely because it eliminates the noise and disturbance incidental to clearing the table and arranging the dining-room after meals, though with suitable doors, glazed or otherwise, and proper draperies between these rooms where they adjoin, this inconvenience is reduced to the minimum.

The economical arrangement of the second floor has been considered quite as carefully as the first, the corners of the house having been utilized as far as possible for sleeping-rooms, thus insuring cross-ventilation and the greatest degree of comfort in warm weather.

DESCRIPTION OF PLANS

The closet space in connection with each room is ample. The baths and linen closets are conveniently located, and in every case the space occupied by halls is a very small percentage of the total area. Where it is desired that certain sleeping-rooms should be larger than shown, it will be found in a majority of these plans that by omitting a partition between two of the smaller rooms this result may easily be obtained.

STYLE

The accompanying illustrations clearly show that the collection of houses contained in this book embraces a great variety of styles; in fact there are no two designs that conflict in any way. In every case unlimited care has been devoted to accurately interpreting the style represented. All of the details have been well studied, much more time having been devoted to each house than would have been possible in the cases of individual clients. The requirements of home-builders are so diversified, and local conditions governing building sites so extreme, that a great range of style is necessary for the success of a book of this type. A Southern Colonial house, for example, would not appear to advantage on the shores of a lake, with a wild, rugged, natural setting; neither could a Swiss châlet be appropriately situated along the main street of a thriving town; but reverse this order and it will be seen that both of these houses will accept their environment in a most natural and graceful manner.

The English half-timber and plain stucco houses have probably a greater range of adaptability than most of the other examples. Not only are they suitable, because of their distinctive characteristics and pleasing composition, to occupy ordinary building lots in the residential sections of smaller cities, as well as in suburban communities, but they are also designed with the idea of filling the requirements of a prospective home-builder who seeks the seclusion of a larger estate, where the possibilities of well-conceived landscape effects will prove a most appropriate and desirable setting as well as greatly emphasizing their attractive features.

The Colonial houses, as well as the American cottage type (or free translation of the Colonial) are always appropriate as country or village residences, and, when properly executed, possess a charm which appeals to every home-lover. A sufficient diversity of designs in this type have been included to enable the most fastidious to make a selection.

The Italian villa and the Spanish Mission house are worthy of special comment. The examples included accurately portray the spirit and architectural characteristics of their respective styles. It will be seen from the illustrations following that these houses possess decided individuality, and for one who wishes to depart from the rather hackneyed models, more attractive results than are afforded by these designs would be difficult to obtain.

The working drawings of each house may be obtained as shown, but the authors advise prospective builders that if the positions of the building sites necessitate a reversal of the plans, they should so instruct their contractors. In most localities, one side of the living-room should face south, as generally the prevailing winds in warm weather are from this quarter, and one side of the dining-room should face east so that in winter this room receives the morning sun. In summer the sun is so high by breakfast time that it does not shine directly into the room. A dining-room with west windows is not a pleasant room. In summer the hot afternoon sun streams through these windows and makes it very uncomfortable for those at the table. In winter the sun has long been down by dinner time.

The plans admit of many changes which in no way affect the final result. In one or two of the houses an extra bathroom could easily be obtained by partitioning off the rear hall, and in most of the houses additional rooms are possible in the attic.

DESCRIPTION OF PLANS

The success of the average home depends not so much upon the attractiveness of the preliminary sketches as upon the amount of study devoted to the drawings from which the house is actually erected. The care with which materials are selected, the size, arrangement and treatment of windows, the overhang of eaves, the choice of hardware, the exterior and interior trim, the proportions of archways and door openings—in fact every detail necessary for the completion of the house, must be carefully considered to produce the best possible results. The authors of this work, realizing the importance of detail in the execution of these designs, have devoted much time and study to each house, and feel assured that in every case where the drawings are accurately followed the results will be eminently satisfactory.

A number of the designs included in this series have found favor with the home-builder even before the actual publication of this book, and such examples as are sufficiently far advanced at the time this volume goes to press will be illustrated by photographs, even though the planting, grading and other desirable settings, as well as the softening effect of occupancy, are missing.

There is probably no one feature of a house that bears so conspicuously important a relationship to both the exterior and interior as does the treatment of windows. The windows in a majority of the homes are shown divided into lights by sash-bars. This undoubtedly gives a richness, sparkle and scale obtainable in no other way. Many people, however, object to this treatment and the bars may be left out. This division into lights is absolutely necessary in the English half-timber and Colonial designs. It is so characteristic of these styles that if omitted the appearance of the houses would suffer greatly. A compromise is to divide only the upper half of double-hung windows and leave the lower half clear glass.

Where perspective drawings are shown, great care has been taken to make them accurate. They show exactly how the houses look from the points at which the perspectives are taken, and are absolutely reliable as to heights and sizes of windows, porches, doors, etc. In each case where casement windows are shown the double-hung type may be substituted, or vice versa. All changes should be settled upon with the builder before a contract is signed, and incorporated in the specifications, which are drawn with optional clauses, the clauses not required being crossed out.

The materials specified are first-class throughout, but here again an option is allowed the home-builder. The most desirable is specified first and optional clauses follow. Shingles may replace clapboards and siding, or the reverse. Foundation walls may be of stone, brick or concrete, depending upon which is the cheapest in the locality where the house is to be built. Stucco probably gives the best results on a masonry wall such as terra cotta blocks, brick or stone, but when so used great care must be taken to thoroughly wet down the walls before applying the stucco. If used on frame, satisfactory work will be obtained by following the specifications closely.

The fireplaces are designed to burn either wood or coal; if the latter, a coal-grate is placed in the opening and the ash-chutes to the cellar do away with carrying ashes through the house.

In the matter of stock hardware it is safe to say that a large percentage of this material on the market to-day is not entirely satisfactory in either design or workmanship. At the same time there is enough that is good to fit the requirements of each house in this series, and the acquirement of appropriate material is simply a question of individual selection.

The subject of lighting fixtures is somewhat more difficult because of the greater range in price. An allowance may be made in the specification to cover this item, but it is advisable that each prospective builder should personally choose the fixtures that are to be used in his house, the variation in cost being a matter of adjustment between the owner and the contractor.

Plumbing fixtures form another item in which the range of selection is very great, and they surely merit the careful consideration of the owner.

The subject of interior finish and decoration is of such unlimited scope, especially when it embraces twenty-one distinctly different houses, that the authors would prefer to advise each prospective home-builder as to the treatment of the house he may select to build, if such advice is desired.

LANDSCAPE WORK

It is difficult to emphasize too strongly the importance of devoting time and study to the arrangement of the walks, planting, etc., in connection with any country home. There is no lot too small to be worthy of such consideration, as frequently the garden spot of a whole community will be found in an area of very small dimensions. An accompanying plate shows the possible formal treatment of the grounds around one of the houses of this series. On this plate the house is shown occupying two positions on a corner lot, the dimensions of which are 50 x 100 ft., and the arrangement of the garden, service yard, garage, etc., represent the natural result of existing requirements. The plate also shows the possibility of reversing any one of the plans in order to conform with local conditions.

MINOR CHANGES AND SPECIAL WORK

Should local conditions require slight changes in the plans other than those that may be taken care of by the contractor, a nominal charge will be made for such service.

Should the individual requirements of a prospective home-builder demand radical changes necessitating the entire reconstruction of the plans of a house, special arrangements may be made with the authors for the execution of this work.

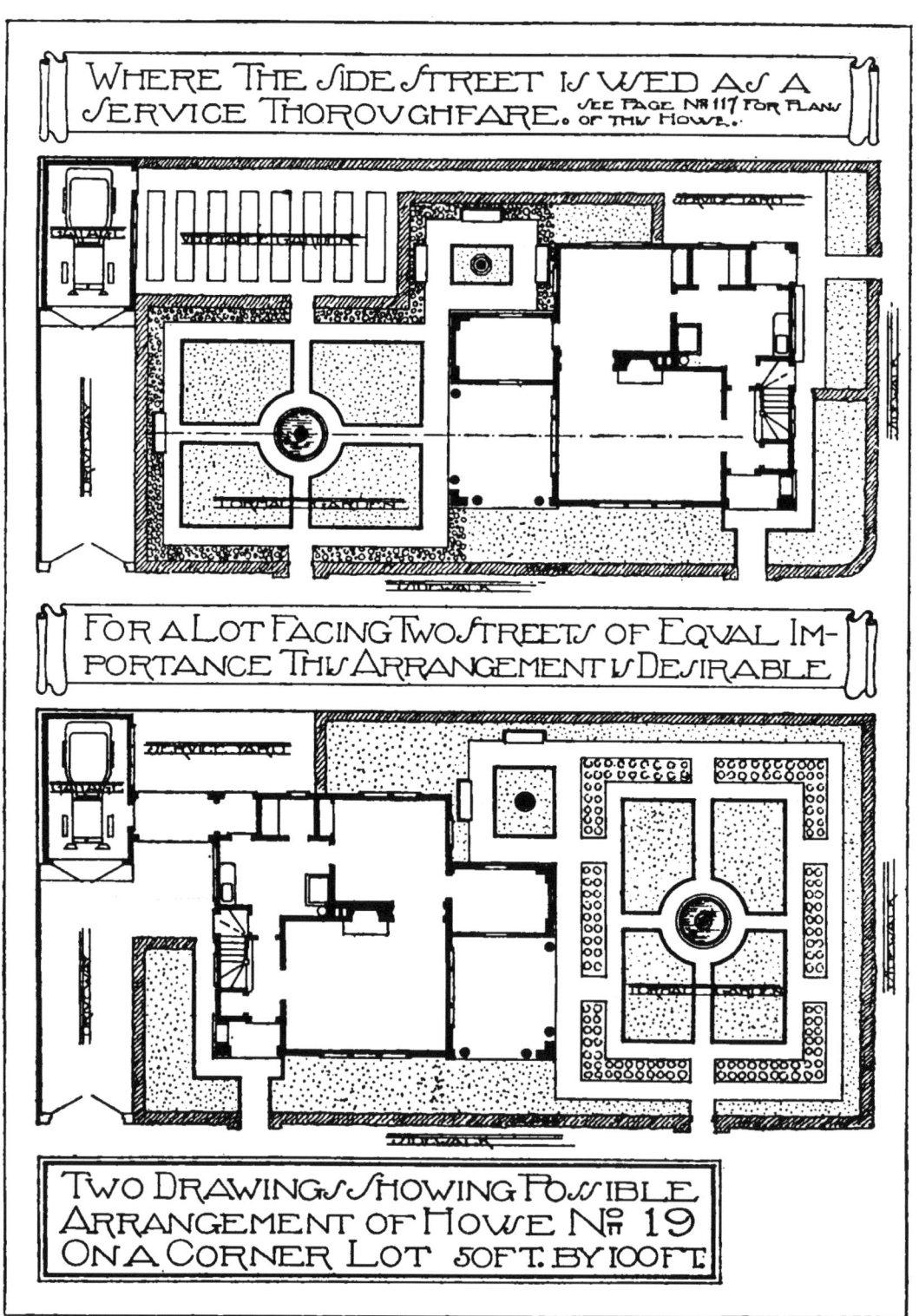

DESCRIPTION OF PLANS

THE PLANS

Three complete sets of working drawings, two specifications and blank contracts are provided for each of the designs illustrated, and these may be obtained at a nominal charge upon application to the publishers, McBride, Nast & Company, Union Square North, New York City. The drawings include the usual quarter-inch plans, elevations and sections; large-scale drawings of special features and full-size details. The specifications are complete, with optional clauses permitting a certain amount of freedom in the choice of materials, etc. One set of the drawings, intended to be used on the work, is printed on cloth, as an ordinary paper set soon wears out or is torn so badly as to be illegible.

Unusual care has been taken in the preparation of these working drawings and specifications to make them so full in detail and explicit in every way that the resulting buildings, at the hands of a reasonably competent contracting builder, will have that air of finished design that belongs to the very best class of specially designed house architecture.

COST

MANY people are apt to be skeptical about the usual magazine articles relating to the cost of small country houses. We daresay that in the majority of cases the magazines are correct, for they publish information regarding an actual house built in some one section of the country. However, the fact that the house is located in *one* section is responsible for the misunderstanding upon the part of the readers.

It is impossible to give a figure that would cover the cost for the entire country. We must consider each factor that enters into the total outlay and judge of its relative importance in the various sections in which building is carried on.

The two principal factors are labor and material. In some places the first factor, labor, plays the more important part. Wages are high and hours are short. For example: in the vicinity of New York City, union labor is well organized, and the mechanics receive the maximum wage for the minimum number of hours. In central and western New York State, carpenters and masons get a modest wage, but some materials, requiring a long haul, are expensive. The lumber sections of the Northwest and some parts of the South give a plentiful supply of cheap material, and where labor's demands are not exorbitant at the same time, we find the most favorable conditions in which to build cheaply.

The distance which material is hauled is a strong factor in determining its cost to the consumer. Therefore, aside from esthetic reasons, it is always wiser to construct your house with materials that are, as far as possible, native to the locality.

In spite of the growing price of woods and the reduction in the price of masonry material, such as cement, it is still cheaper to build

COST

a frame house than one of any other kind. Of course certain parts favored with the close proximity of brick-yards or quarries give these materials the advantage over frame on account of durability and cheapness.

To get down to facts, we shall compare the prices obtained from each quarter of the country; prices obtained on the same house and specifications. The house illustrated as Design No. 4 was selected as being fairly representative of a moderate-size dwelling presenting no particular difficulties of construction or detail. Plans, elevations and specifications were sent to architects throughout the United States and Canada asking for information as to the cost of this particular house in each locality. The resulting estimates, as had been expected, varied greatly in accord with local conditions regarding labor and materials. Summarized, they are as follows, lump-sum costs being given, together with a comparison of costs per cubic foot of house in various materials:—

New York City Suburbs ....$4300.
    per cubic foot, frame ....17 cents
    per cubic foot, brick ....$21\frac{1}{2}$ cents
    per cubic foot, stone ....$22\frac{1}{2}$ cents
    stucco on metal lath ....18 cents

Philadelphia Suburbs 10% to 15% less than near New York.

Maine ....$3400.
    per cubic foot, frame ....14 cents
    per cubic foot, brick ....17 cents
    per cubic foot, stone ....20 cents
    stucco on metal lath ....15 cents

In the southern New England States the cost would be slightly in excess of the above.

Middle South, Kentucky, Maryland, etc. ....$3000.

  per cubic foot, frame .... 10 to 12 cents
  per cubic foot, brick .... 12 to 14 cents
  per cubic foot, stone .... 15 to 20 cents
  stucco on metal lath .... 11 to 14 cents

Chicago, vicinity of .... $3800.
  per cubic foot, frame .... 15 to 16 cents
  per cubic foot, brick .... 18 cents
  per cubic foot, stone .... 20 cents
  stucco on metal lath .... 16 to 17 cents

Middle-western States such as Ohio, Michigan, Iowa
  and Wisconsin .... $2550 to $4000.
  per cubic foot, frame .... 10 to 17 cents
  per cubic foot, brick .... 12½ to 20 cents
  per cubic foot, stone .... 16 to 25 cents up
  stucco on metal lath .... 12 to 18 cents up

Pacific coast (Northwest) .... $2000 to $3200.
  per cubic foot, frame .... 8½ to 13 cents
  per cubic foot, brick .... 9½ to 14 cents
  per cubic foot, stone .... 14 to 16 cents
  stucco on metal lath .... 9 to 14 cents

Colorado (average) .... $3100 to $3200.
  per cubic foot, frame .... 12 cents
  per cubic foot, brick .... 14 cents
  per cubic foot, stone .... 15 cents
  stucco on metal lath .... 13 cents

Southwest (Arizona and New Mexico) .... $2900 to $3000.
  per cubic foot, frame .... 12 cents
  per cubic foot, brick .... 13½ to 14 cents
  per cubic foot, stone .... 16 cents
  stucco on metal lath .... 13½ to 14 cents

  We have covered in the above list a wide range of territory. The

New York section heads the list, with the Northwest Pacific Coast at the foot, due to the peculiar conditions mentioned above. Prices, however, may vary in each section. We have known of two houses built from the same plans and specifications, one in Flushing, Long Island, and the other in Essex County, New Jersey, in which the cost at Flushing was 10 per cent. less than on the Jersey coast. Transportation had much to do with this variation.

In giving a scale of prices such as above it was necessary to take as a basis a certain type of house; this is one which includes all the conveniences and arrangements suitable for the average family without any special features or elaborate details. The construction is supposed to be thorough and materials first-class. It is simply a good substantial home, built according to the custom of the locality for a house of this class. These figures are for a completed house with the exception of the lighting fixtures, which may cost any amount one is willing to pay. They could be procured for $50 as a minimum.

Everyone, about to build, is desirous of first ascertaining as nearly as possible, the total outlay he will be obliged to make. The first step after selecting the design is to multiply the total cubic contents as given with each design by the cost per cubic foot in your section. You will then be able to get an idea if it is possible to keep within your appropriation. Next consult a local builder—one who is accustomed to putting up the class of building you desire. There may be certain governing conditions in your neighborhood with which he is familiar and you are not. He will take the cubical contents and the design as illustrated, together with instructions as to how you wish the house finished, and give you a very close preliminary estimate. Then when he receives the working drawings, details and complete specifications his figure may be gone over and verified. Of course, if the builder has the final drawings at the outset, he will be able to give at once an exact and final figure.

If you contemplate building a home, study your own section.

What, in the long run, seem to have proven to be the best materials for the locality? What materials are used for foundation walls, exterior walls, roofs, porches, trim, chimneys, etc.? If one material predominates for each part, then there is some good reason why it was used—probably for the sake of economy or procurability. A little thought and careful study in the beginning may save time and expense in the end.

THE DESIGNS

A VACATION HOME

DESIGN NO. 1

THIS type of house is admirably adapted to seaside or mountainous country as a summer cottage. Rather wild and rugged scenery will make the best setting for this simple structure.

The arrangement of the first floor plan, with its combined living-room and dining-room opening on either side through wide French windows upon two roomy porches, will give an effect of space and open air freedom most desirable for summer use. A separate entrance is provided, convenient to both living-room and kitchen, chiefly for use in stormy weather and for the reception of formal guests. A pantry separates the living-room from the kitchen which latter is provided with a large store-room and a special service porch.

The second floor is divided into four rooms, two large and two small, a bath, and ample linen closet, as well as spacious closets in each of the rooms. The cellar contains a laundry with two stationary tubs, a store-room for vegetables, etc. Provision is made for a boiler and two coal compartments. The former can be installed at the discretion of the owner and will be necessary only if the house is used in the early spring and late fall.

The house is frame throughout and is designed to have either siding or shingles on the exterior walls. These should have a wide spacing and if painted white with a stained shingle roof, a pleasing contrast will be obtained. The cellar walls may be built of stone, brick or concrete, depending upon the procurability of these materials. The finish of the living-room is an important considera-

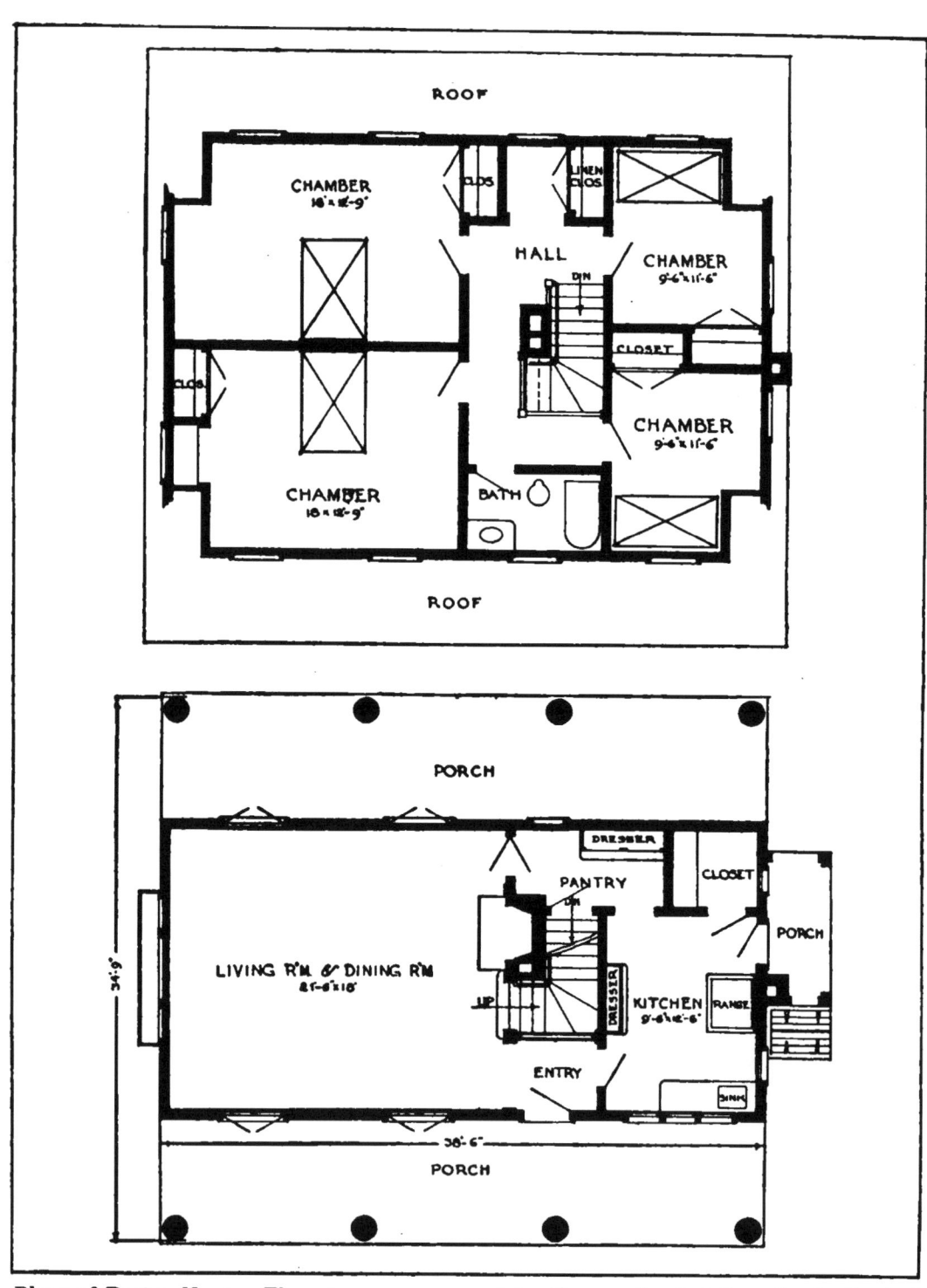

Plans of Design No. 1. There is more space upstairs than on the first floor due to the fact that the second-story rooms are built partly out over the porch.

Perspective view of Design No. 1. The long porch on either side of the building suggests its character of summer home upon practically any type of site. The exterior walls are designed for either siding or shingles

A VACATION HOME

tion. No doubt white is pleasing and cheerful, but for rough wear in the country, a dark, natural wood treatment will be found more durable. The specifications of this house allow for both treatments. The bedrooms are finished in white. If the exterior is white then paint the blinds a light green, but remember that in doing so, green fades out, therefore make the final coat a bit darker than the color you ultimately wish.

To secure the best exposures, the end of the living-room with the triple window, may face either east, south or west. This will give good cross ventilation in hot weather.

While this house does excellently for a rugged landscape, it would stand a bit of planting and gardening around it. Shrubs and cedars here have an appropriate background.

This cottage should cost in the neighborhood of $8,000 but in many localities may come considerably under this figure. Consult your builder about the cost per cubic foot or square foot of ground area, for a house of this type. The plan area is 886 sq. ft. and the total cubical contents is 21,264 cubic feet.

AN ENGLISH STUCCO COTTAGE

DESIGN NO. 2

THE great charm of this house lies in the fact that it embraces all the salient features of a much larger and more pretentious home, so thoroughly condensed and economically arranged that its construction is possible for a very moderate sum. The elevations (designed in the purest type of English cottage architecture, harmoniously combined with the porch, which in this country is so essential) all possess attractive lines and the house may be viewed with satisfaction from any point. It is therefore a most appropriate design for a corner lot or an estate embracing many acres.

The excellent arrangement of the rooms may be seen by examining the plans which are illustrated on the following page. The relationship of the dining-room to the living-room gives a long and pleasing vista which naturally increases the apparent size of both rooms. The French windows leading from the dining-room to the porch allow the latter to be used as an outdoor dining-room, which is most desirable in hot weather. The opening between the living-room and dining-room may be left without doors or it may be provided with glazed doors—always an attractive feature. The kitchen is removed from the living quarters but is very convenient to the dining-room and entrance hall and connects with the second story by a service stairway. The second floor gives the three principal chambers across the front with a servant's room and toilet entirely apart from the master's quarters. Notice the exceptionally good closet space in this house. The first floor has a coat closet, pantry and store-

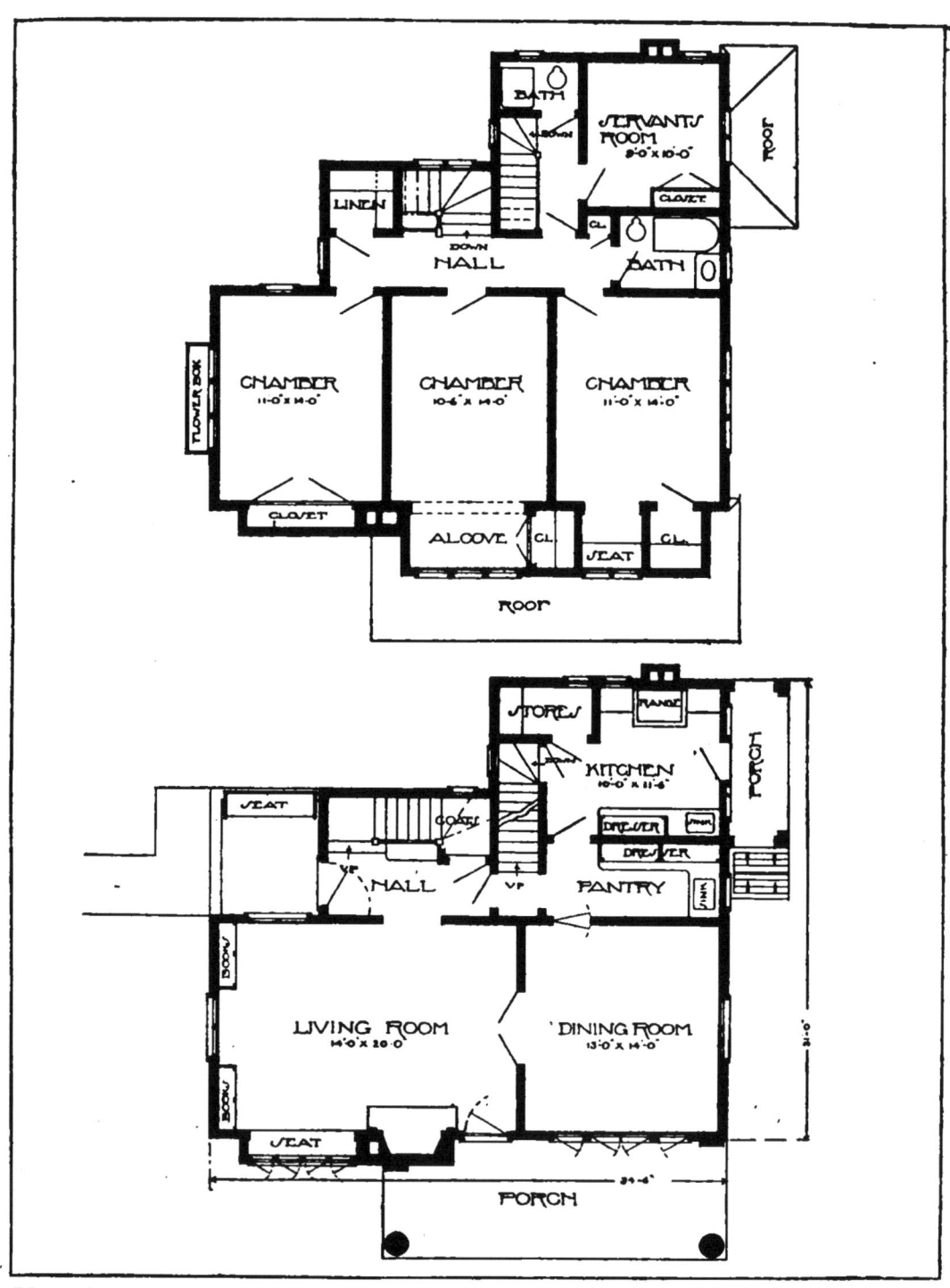

Plan of Design No. 2. The relationship of the dining-room and living-room, extending entirely across the front of the house, gives a long and pleasing vista which increases the apparent size of both rooms.

Perspective view of Design No. 2. There are few types of architecture that so readily impress one with a sense of their homelikeness as does the English cottage type in stucco. This house is so designed as to be attractive from all four sides

room. Each bedroom has a generous closet and there is a large linen closet, while near the bathroom is a small broom closet. The width of the porch could easily be increased three or four feet by giving the roof a more gradual sweep from the dormer down; a very slight additional cost would cover this change if made during the course of erection. The cellar provides for a laundry with stationary tubs, storeroom for vegetables, etc., and a heater with two coal compartments.

The house is of frame construction with a stucco finish and shingle roof. The foundation may be either stone, brick or concrete, with a concrete cellar floor. The principal first floor rooms have hardwood floors and the finish may be either white throughout or in natural woods, such as oak, chestnut or cypress. A beamed ceiling in the living-room would be most appropriate if a natural wood should be selected for the first floor finish, and the extra cost would probably not exceed $50.

The house as drawn may have the long side face either east or south. Both positions give one side of the dining-room to the east and one side of the living-room to the south, which is the best exposure for these rooms.

Stucco walls offer an ideal background for vines. A lattice design is placed around the living-room window for this purpose and the flower-box above will add to the general color effect. A few dark evergreens close up to the walls under the other living-room window will be a great help. The combination of garden walks and hedges is most pleasing with this type of house.

The cost of this house is from $4,500 to $5,500, depending upon the locality. For comparison with other designs the floor plan has 936 sq. ft. of ground area and the whole building contains 24,886 cu. ft.

A MODIFIED DUTCH COLONIAL TYPE

DESIGN NO. 3

HERE is a modified Colonial cottage resembling in its general exterior characteristics Design No. 1, though possessing a much more formal treatment of the place. This house, intended primarily for summer use, is so arranged that it will serve the purpose of an all-the-year house with perfect satisfaction. In a community where each land-owner possesses a tract of land of an acre or more, this house would prove a picturesque and pleasing example of rural architecture. And for compactness of plan and convenience of its general arrangement, it will doubtless prove more livable than many more elaborate houses.

On the ground floor an entrance hall of liberal dimensions leads both into the living-room and dining-room and also connects with the kitchen. The living-room and dining-room are connected by a wide opening containing glazed doors which, with proper draperies, are as efficacious as solid doors and far preferable. The fireplace, on the axis with the door to the dining-room, will prove as effective in that room as though a separate fireplace had been placed there. In connection with the kitchen will be found the necessary store-closet, pantry and service porch. On the second floor the least possible amount of hall space has been utilized to obtain comfortable access to the four sleeping-rooms, each of which is provided with ample closet room. A bathroom and linen closet complete the equipment.

The cellar provides room for the usual compartments for coal, a boiler space, store-room, wash trays and servants' toilet.

To return to the plan, we notice the excellent seclusion of the service portion of the establishment. While the kitchen is very con-

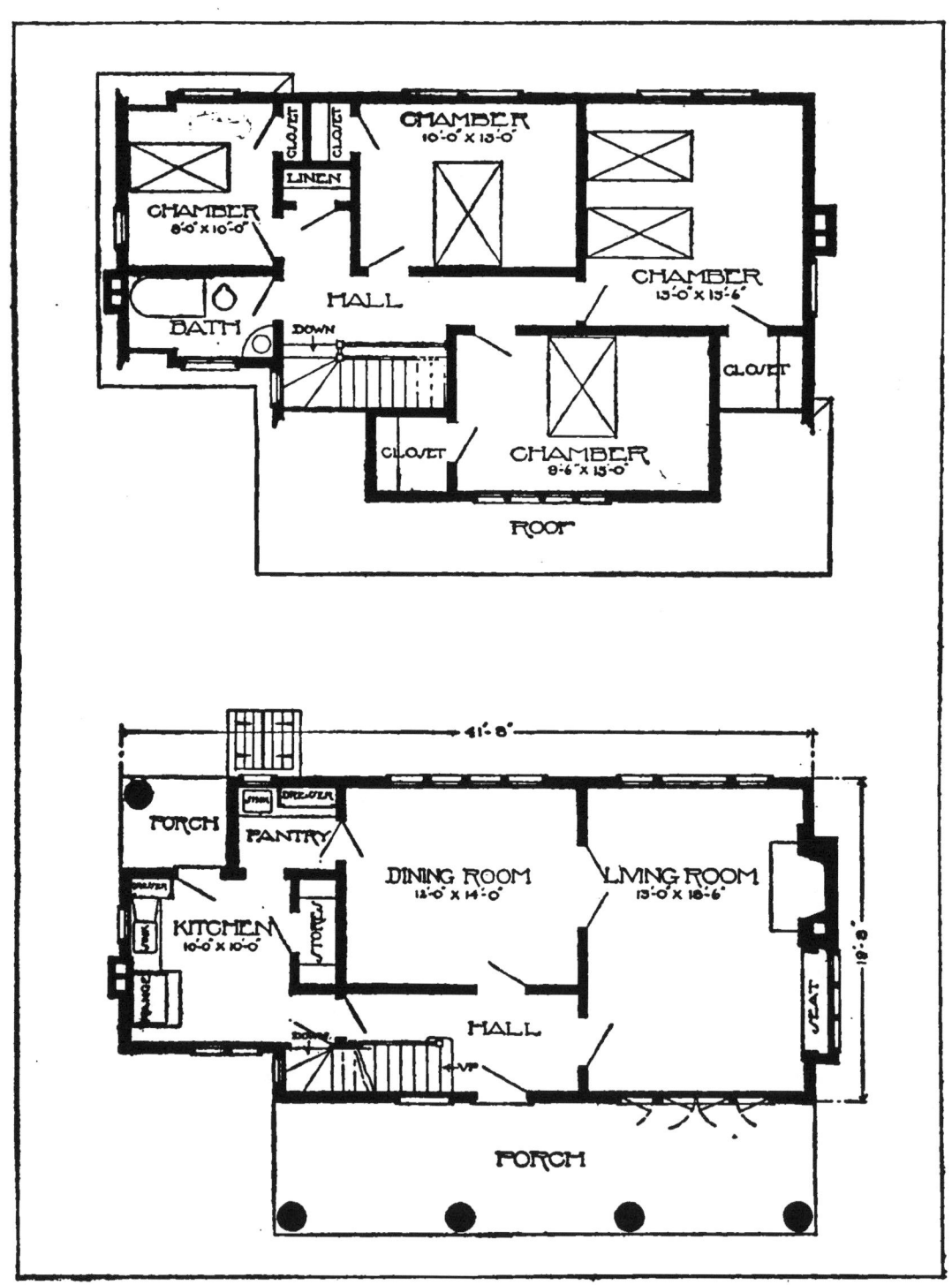

Plans of Design No. 3. An unusually small amount of space has been given up to the hall, although not at the sacrifice of convenient intercommunication.

Perspective view of Design No. 3. This house was designed primarily as a summer home but there is no reason why it could not be adapted with perfect satisfaction to be used as an all-the-year house

DUTCH COLONIAL TYPE

venient to both the dining-room and the front entrance, yet it may be effectively shut off from these parts and any work going on there need not interfere with the life in the living portions, such as the veranda and large living-room.

Undoubtedly the exterior will look best if the shingles, or clapboards if used, are laid with a generous expanse to the weather. This will increase the apparent length of the house by making the horizontal lines more pronounced.

Two color schemes occur to us, both suitable for this house. First, paint all the exterior white, i. e., sash, side walls, columns, trim, etc., with the exception of the lattice, which may be a light green. Then with the roof left to weather or stained either dull red or moss green, a sparkling and cheery effect is obtained. The other scheme is to stain the side walls, if of shingles, a silvery gray and paint all exterior woodwork white, with the roof as above described. This, while not quite as brilliant as the other scheme, is well suited to a more exposed situation. The best exposure for this plan arrangement is to face the long side of the living-room south. This will give the prevailing winds in summer access to this room and also bring the sun into the dining-room during the breakfast hour.

The ground area covered by this house is 780 square feet and its cubical contents approximately 19,500 cubic feet. The average cost would be from $3300 to $3500.

A COLONIAL HOUSE FOR A VILLAGE STREET

DESIGN NO. 4

HERE is a simple Colonial house of the Northern type suitable for a village street or a small farm in the rural districts. The spirit and character of the working drawings will be found to be correct, and for anyone having a predilection for Colonial architecture this house will surely prove a satisfactory investment. The elevations shown in connection with the plans are taken directly from the quarter-inch scale working drawings, omitting the structural features, dimensions, etc.

On the first floor plan it will be seen that a large living-room and the dining-room, connected by glazed doors and both opening upon a porch running the depth of the house, form a very attractive suite for the living quarters. The entrance hall communicates directly with the service quarters which consist of kitchen, store-room and porch. On the second floor are three corner chambers, two of which are exceptionally large and all having ample closet room, bath and linen closet. In the attic is space for a small finished room and store-room. The cellar provides for a laundry with stationary tubs, servants' toilet, store-room for vegetables, etc., and a heater with two coal compartments.

The side walls of this house will look best of clapboards or siding. They should be laid eight or nine inches to the weather, and provision is made for this in the specifications.

Two colors go well on the side walls; either white or a dull yellow. In both cases the trim, sash, entrance, columns and railing are best

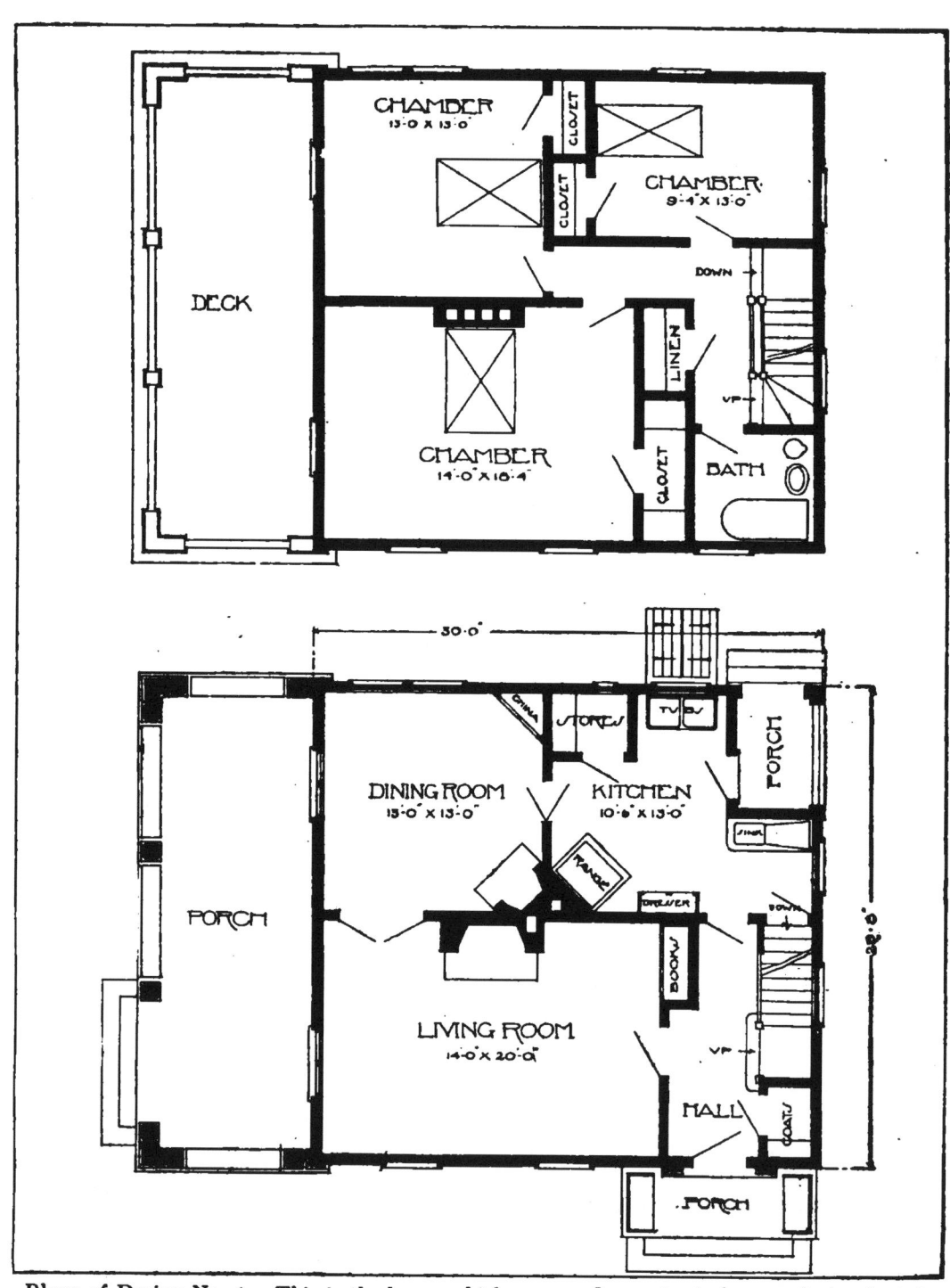

Plans of Design No. 4. This is the house which was used as a typical example in obtaining the data set forth in the chapter on Cost, page 18. The square plan is always economical.

Front and end elevations of Design No. 4. Clapboards or siding would make the best exterior wall covering for this house, laid with as wide an expanse to the weather as possible—eight or nine inches if this can be secured

in white. If the side walls are yellow then paint the shutters white also. You will be surprised at the charming effect thus obtained. If, however, the side walls are white, then finish the shutters in a dull apple green. The chimney may be either red brick or stone.

For the interior of a Colonial house, no color goes as well as white. A simple and pleasing treatment would be to use white throughout, with the exception of the kitchen. This may be a cool neutral color. The typical mahogany hand-rail and newels, with white balusters and dark stair treads, are quite necessary in following out the style.

The best exposure for the front of the house is east. This places the porch on the south side and makes the living-room cool in summer and warm in winter. It also brings the rooms not used for living on the north side. As this plan is designed to fit a narrow lot, the exposure may be determined in advance by the size of the plot which admits of but one position. It may be necessary in that case to reverse the plan. This any intelligent builder can do.

The ground area is 855 square feet, and the approximate contents 24,795 cubic feet. The cost is from $3800 to $4000.

AN ITALIAN VILLA

DESIGN NO. 5

NOTHING could be more pleasing and worthy of comment than this miniature Italian villa. The Italian influence is felt in nearly all of the best of the larger recent architectural achievements in this country and there is no reason why simple, beautifully proportioned examples of Italian domestic architecture of a few centuries ago should not serve as inspirations for our more modest homes of the present day. Notwithstanding the limited dimensions of this house, it could not be more nearly complete if it were four times as large, which would only mean the increased size of the existing rooms together with a few additional sleeping-rooms.

The stairs, screened from the living-room by curtains, are accessible both from the living quarters and service quarters. The dining-room, living-room and porch form the living quarters, while in connection with the kitchen will be found a pantry, store-room and service porch. On the second floor there are three sleeping-rooms, good closet room, a bath and linen closet, also a hall of fair dimensions which could be furnished and used as a sitting-room. This hall opens upon the loggia which may be used as a sleeping-porch. The cellar provides for a laundry with stationary tubs, servants' toilet, store-room for vegetables, etc., and a heater with two coal compartments.

It would be inadvisable to make the stucco of an Italian house any color but of the lightest tints. A cream color with a rather smooth finish would be appropriate for this design. The trim and columns must be white, for we can count on the roof and shutters for

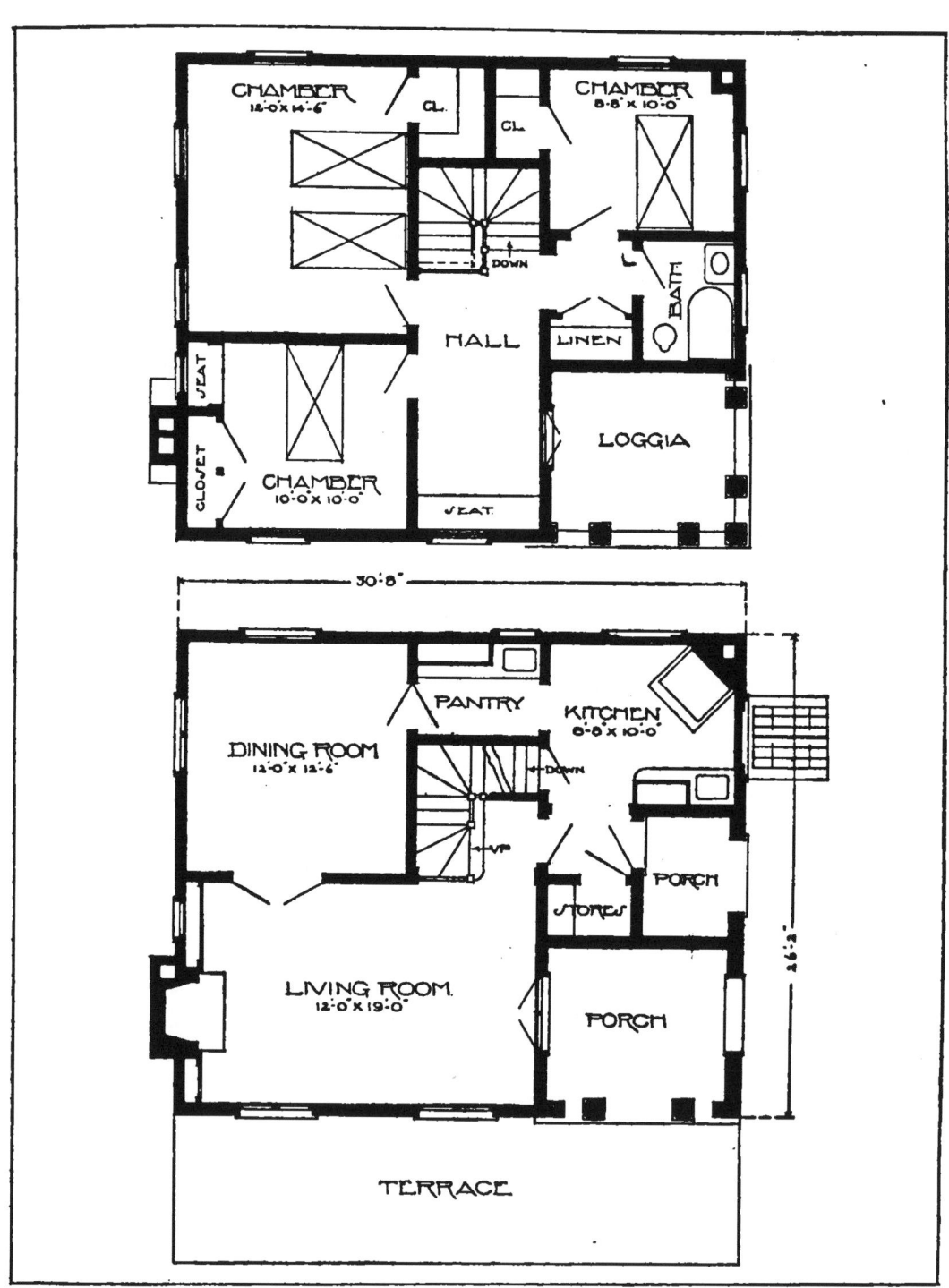

Plans of Design No. 5. The stairs may be screened from the living-room by curtains if desired. The uncovered terrace across the front is eight feet wide.

Perspective view of Design No. 5. The Italian style of house is one that is very closely associated with concrete and stucco walls by reason of the fact that in its original environment the fundamental features of the design naturally evolved from the use of these materials

our color notes. If the roof is tile, use the red S-tiles and if shingles, stain them red. The shutters are a light washed-out green. They should not be dark, for in that case they would make a discordant note.

The living-room may well be treated with a dark stain, something like Italian walnut. This same treatment may be carried out for the remainder of the first floor rooms, and even for bedrooms if wished. However, here as in the other designs, white is perhaps the more satisfactory.

West will be found the best direction in which to face this house. This will give the breezes, in most localities, on the porch and loggia side and the morning sun in the dining-room and kitchen.

A bit of garden in the Italian style will give this villa an excellent setting. Remember, however, that Italian gardens were designed primarily to live in, not merely to look into. By keeping this in mind a more successful result will be obtained.

The ground area is 7460 square feet and the contents approximately 20,888 cubic feet. The cost will range from $4000 to $4500.

A STUCCO BUNGALOW

DESIGN NO. 6

THE photograph on the page following shows this bungalow in a state nearing completion, so of course the effects of planting and grading, as well as the softening tones of occupancy are missing. The exterior walls of the house are of stucco, the roof shingled and the chimney, stone, producing a very pleasing combination. A living-room, dining-room, kitchen and three chambers constitute the six main rooms. Aside from them a store-room, linen closet, coat closet, bath and ample closet room for each chamber will be found. A large living-porch and servants' porch complete the first floor layout. It will be noticed, upon reference to the plan, that the bedrooms and bath have been kept entirely separate from the living-room, dining-room and kitchen, being reached from these latter through the two doorways shown. This desirable separation of living quarters from the sleeping-rooms is one of the most difficult things to secure in a practical bungalow plan. There is a cellar, providing for a laundry with stationary tubs, a servants' toilet, store-room for vegetables, and a heater with two coal compartments.

The color scheme for the exterior of this bungalow should be light gray stucco with white woodwork. This, together with a weathered shingle roof and stone chimneys, will produce a very harmonious effect.

A setting of large trees as shown in the photograph will add greatly to the charm of this summer home.

The living-room and a dining-room may be treated in natural

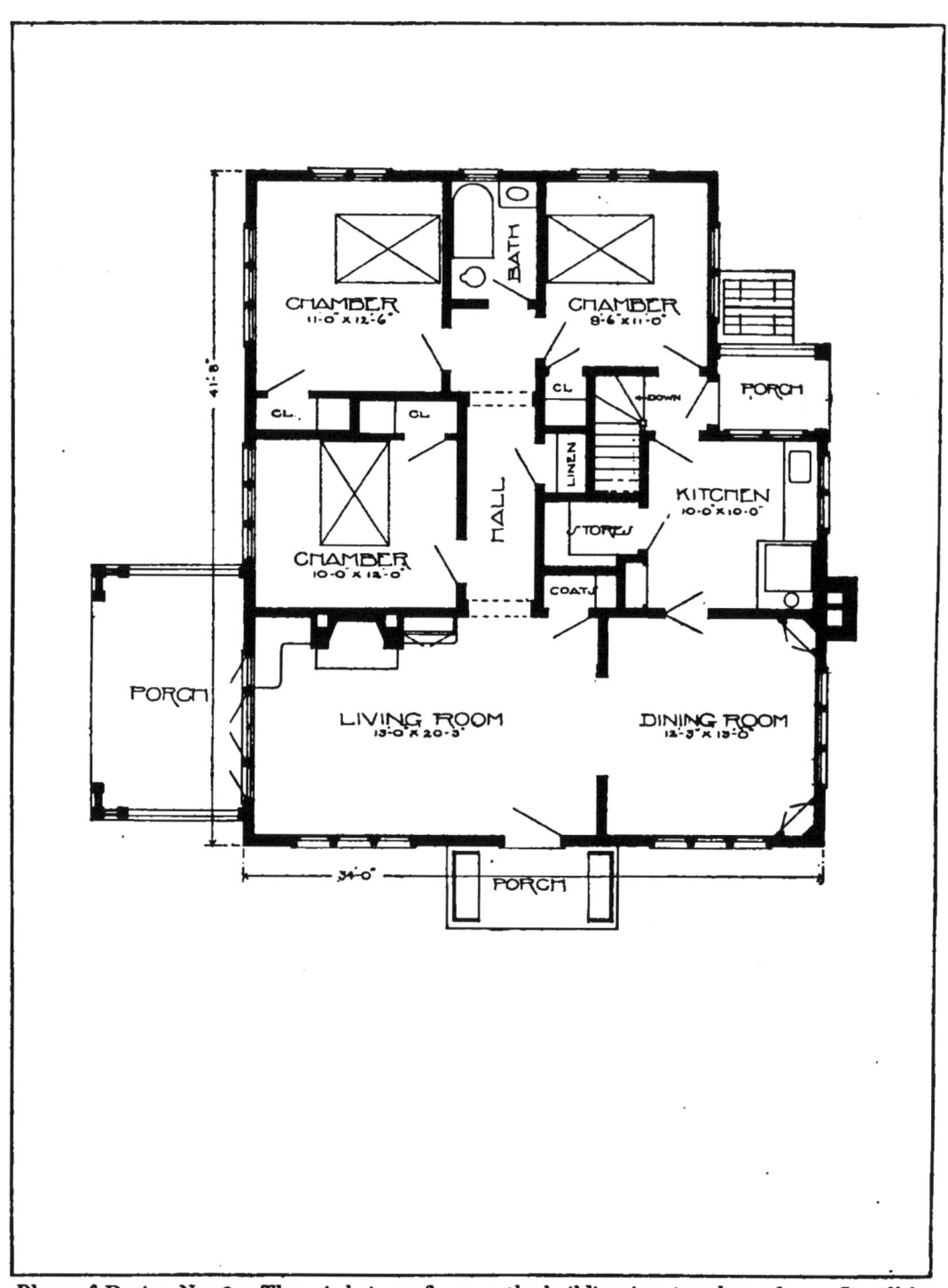

Plans of Design No. 6. There is but one floor, so the building is a true bungalow. It will be noticed that the sleeping-quarters are well isolated from the living-quarters. The combination of living-room and dining-room across the whole front is a very pleasing arrangement.

Design No. 6, from a photograph. A bungalow in stucco is not as yet a very common sight, though there is no particular reason why this most adaptable material should not be utilized in the one-story house

The entrance porch is not large, merely a small platform with seats sheltered by a vine lattice

woods, and a beamed ceiling in the dining-room would be a most appropriate addition. The sleeping-rooms may either have a painted trim or be natural wood finish and harmonize with the two main rooms.

The plan covers a ground area of 1259 square feet and occupies approximately 20,144 cubic feet of space. The estimated cost is $3600 to $4000.

AN ENGLISH HALF-TIMBER COTTAGE

DESIGN NO. 7

A UNIQUE English half-timber cottage is shown by the drawings, wonderfully well adapted to the requirements of the home-builder who desires a house possessing distinctive characteristics both in plan and elevation, at the same time having limitations as to cost. The elevations have been designed with great care and the window openings have been arranged with the idea of lending as much interest as possible to the simple lines of the house. The roof should have a woven shingle treatment in lieu of the thatched roof, which in this country is not practicable. The boards forming the half-timbering, in fact all the exterior structural woodwork, should be adzed, which softens the lines and gives the effect of hand-hewn timbers.

The plan is interesting because of its simplicity and compactness. A living-room, dining-room and porch form the family quarters on the first floor. Both these rooms open upon the porch and are connected with each other by an archway or door, whichever may be desired. The stairs lead up from the living-room and are also accessible from the kitchen at the first landing. The kitchen is provided with a store-room and service porch. On the second floor are three corner chambers, with ample closet room, bath and linen closet. The cellar provides for a laundry with stationary tubs, a servants' toilet, store-room for vegetables, etc., and a heater with two coal compartments.

In a house of this character the limitations for an artistic interior treatment are almost removed entirely. There are many charming effects to be obtained by the expenditure of comparatively little

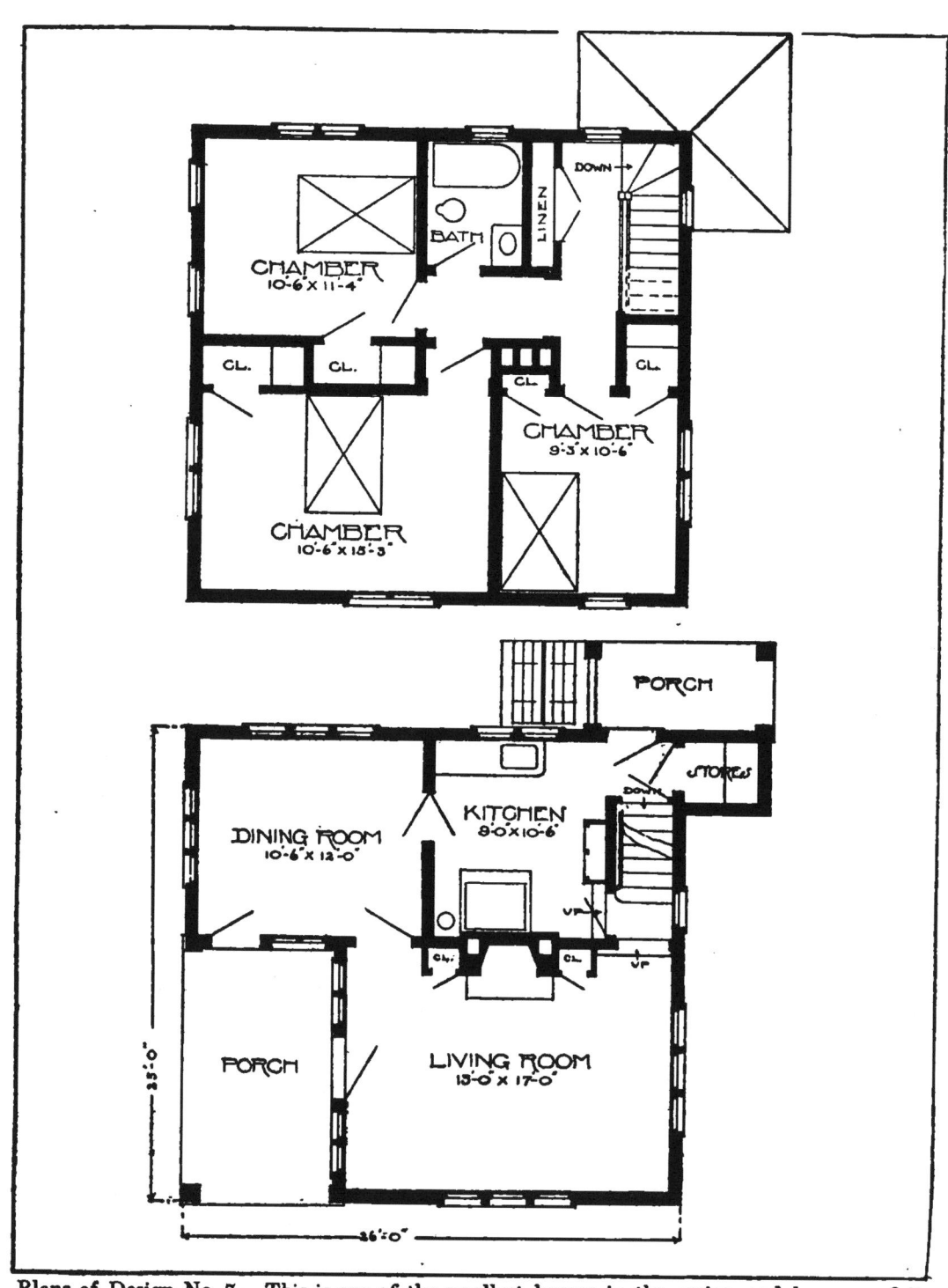

Plans of Design No. 7. This is one of the smallest houses in the series, and because of its square plan could be built very economically.

Perspective view of Design No. 7. A common mistake in the half-timber house is to have too great a contrast in color between the plaster and the woodwork. Another common fault is too great complexity of design in the half-timbering

money. In the living-room a battened wainscot, five feet high, of chestnut, with richly colored plaster walls above, a false beamed ceiling of adzed timber, and a floor of oak, the boards being irregular in width, quaint cupboards built into the wainscoting and a few richly colored Moravian tiles inserted in the breast and hearth of the fireplace, will add greatly to its charm. Reproductions of old English fabrics should be used as draperies, and great care should be taken in the selection of furniture and lighting fixtures. This general treatment should apply to both of the main rooms of the first floor.

The rooms on the second floor should be finished in natural wood with either rough plaster walls, tinted, or characteristic wall papers. Owing to the very simple lines of the house, a certain amount of planting should be done as close to the building as possible, thus easing its somewhat severe lines. Here as in house No. 12 leaded glass should be used in all windows and glazed doors, in which case the sash should be painted lead color. The stucco should be white or gray and the half-timber work brown—light or dark, depending upon the color of the stucco. The roof should be weathered shingles.

This plan covers a ground area of 650 square feet and occupies approximately 17,550 cubic feet of space. The estimated cost is $3000 to $3200.

A SOUTHERN COLONIAL HOUSE

DESIGN NO. 8

THE design presents a very satisfactory example of Southern Colonial architecture as applied to a house of small dimensions. Its merits are apparent in the perspective shown on the page following. The working drawings and details have been studied with the idea of producing a house which will be absolutely correct from the standpoint of style. The body of the house is stucco; the columns, cornices, etc., are wood. On the first floor a large living-room occupies one entire side of the house, having light on three elevations and opening upon a porch which may be enclosed in winter. The dining-room is a corner room with good window space. A porch may be added in connection with this room, corresponding with the porch on the living-room side, making the house symmetrical and not greatly increasing its cost. The main stairs lead up from the living-room and are designed to form a very attractive addition to this room. A door leads from the kitchen to the first stair landing. A service porch and good-sized store-room adjoin the kitchen. On the second floor are four chambers, ample closet space, a bath and linen closet. The cellar provides ample space for a laundry with stationary tubs, a servants' toilet, vegetable room and a heater with two coal compartments.

The interior of this house should be kept as simple as possible and strictly Colonial in detail—the trim white, or with possibly the slightest suggestion of gray, the hand-rail of the stairs as well as the treads, birch stained mahogany. The doors in the main rooms of the first floor, should the owner wish to spend the additional money,

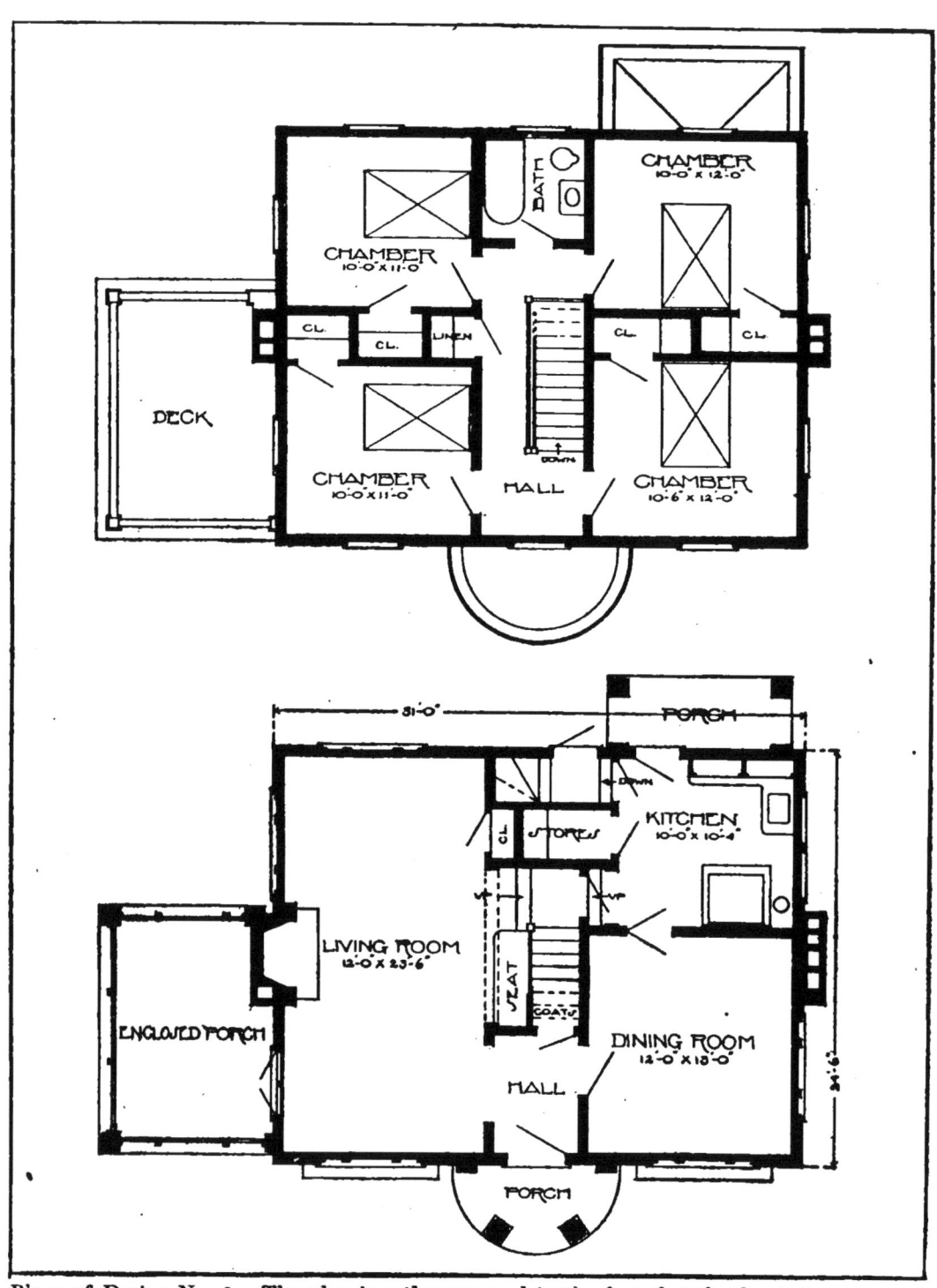

Plans of Design No. 8. The plan is rather unusual in the fact that the front stairs are not visible from the hall. They lead up from the side of the living-room and are joined by a short flight from the kitchen.

Perspective view of Design No. 8. Either before the building is started, or later, another porch might be added at the near end to open off the dining-room, making the house exactly symmetrical in the front

SOUTHERN COLONIAL HOUSE

would produce a very rich effect if made in mahogany with cut-glass doorknobs. The walls of the various rooms could be either papered or treated with a rough plaster finish of a rich brownish yellow—though great care would have to be taken in arriving at the desired color.

The exterior stucco should be pale gray, and all of the exterior woodwork white. The tin roof should be green. A simple treatment of the grounds is suggested in the accompanying illustration. This house may face either west or south to advantage.

This plan covers a ground area of 760 square feet and occupies approximately 22,040 cubic feet of space. The estimated cost is $4400 to $4800.

A SPANISH MISSION TYPE

DESIGN NO. 9

THE Spanish Mission house, rapidly growing in favor with people who appreciate simple, distinctive lines in stucco buildings, will be found illustrated in the following plans and drawings. In this example Mission architecture is suggested, rather than forced upon one, and the free treatment renders it a suitable structure to occupy a position adjacent to buildings quite different in style. This house, preferably constructed of hollow tile or other masonry exterior walls, with red Spanish tile roof, will prove quite as attractive of frame construction. Very pleasing effects may be obtained by substituting a shingle roof for tile, in which case the cost of construction would be materially lessened.

There is not a square inch of waste space in the plans of this house, the minimum amount having been used both on the first and second floors for halls and passages. On the first floor the living-room is entered through an archway at the right of the entrance hall and at the left are the stairs leading to the second floor. A coat closet occupies a convenient position, and the kitchen communicates directly with the entrance hall and stairs through a passageway, which leaves the living-room and dining-room free from any unnecessary intrusion on the part of the servants. These two rooms are well proportioned and the interior treatment simple and effective. On the second floor are four family sleeping-rooms, ample closet room, bath, linen closet and servants' room. In the cellar are found a laundry with stationary tubs, servants' toilet, store-room for vegetables, etc., and a heater with two coal compartments.

A fairly rough white stucco is the proper treatment for the main

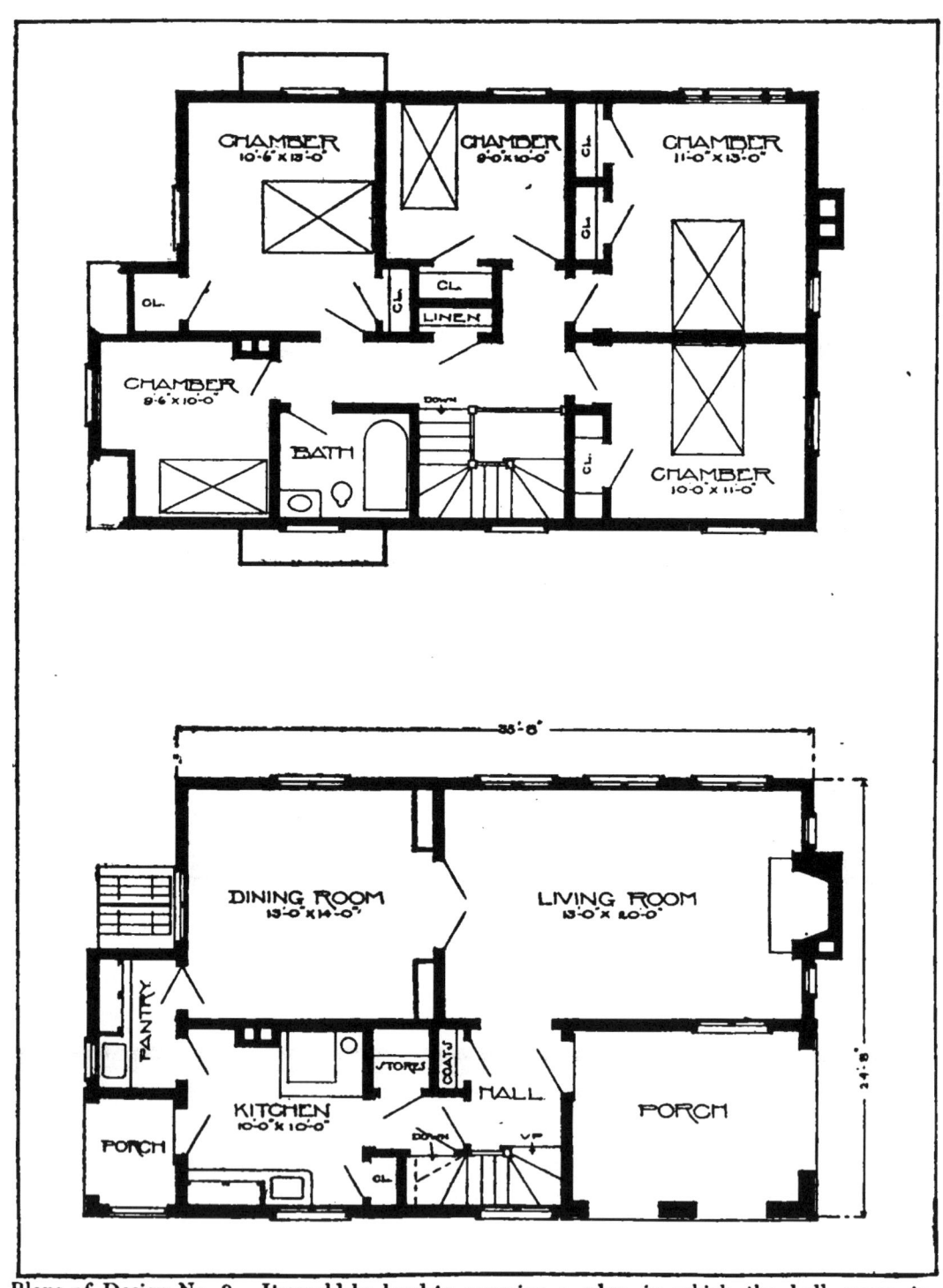

Plans of Design No. 9. It would be hard to conceive a plan in which the hall space is reduced to a smaller proportion of the whole. Every inch of floor space is made to count.

Perspective view of Design No. 9. The most common characteristics of the Spanish Mission type are arched openings through thick walls, iron-work balconies or window guards as a foil to the stucco, and the gable wall with its distinctive coping

body of this house. The roof should, of course, be Spanish tile of a deep rich red, the blinds and exterior trim a faded green of a bluish cast, the sash and sash-bars white. The iron balcony should be painted dark green over the red metallic paint. The porch ceiling could be a very pale blue with good effect, and the porch floor red tile or red brick with gray joints, though of course cement will answer where it is advisable to economize. Two terra cotta flower vases, placed adjacent to the porch piers, will add interest to the house. These may be obtained in most excellent stock designs in various colors at numerous dealers for a nominal sum. This house may face northwest to advantage. Where possible the planting in connection with this house should be of a semi-tropical nature—at any rate the shrubbery about the house should be of as variegated coloring as possible and the garden should contain a great profusion of flowering plants. The walks should be of brick or white gravel.

In this house also, there is an opportunity for future consideration as to the elaboration of the main rooms.

The plan covers a ground area of 966 square feet and occupies approximately 26,082 cubic feet of space. The cost is estimated at from $5000 to $5400.

A STUCCO HOUSE FOR A NARROW LOT

DESIGN NO. 10

THE plans and rendered elevation of this house are offered as an example of a roomy and compact home that can be built economically and effectively on a narrow lot.

The total width of the house proper is 26 feet 6 inches, With outside chimneys as indicated this dimension is increased somewhat, though it is quite possible to build this house with inside chimneys. The regularity of the rooms, however, through which the chimneys pass, will be affected by their inclusion within the walls.

The elevations as shown indicate stucco walls with a shingle roof, though shingles or clapboards may be substituted for stucco with very pleasing results.

Examination of the plans will make clear the fact that they are particularly well studied. On the first floor the intercommunicating living-room and dining-room produce an attractive vista, the total length from front of living-room to dining-room bay being 34 feet 6 inches. The kitchen communicates directly with the entrance hall and with the dining-room through the butler's pantry. The dining-room, with its bay-window and four corner-cupboards running to the ceiling, is most attractive and unusual. The living-room is well proportioned and has a large fireplace and ample wall space. There is a roomy coat closet in the entrance hall and in connection with the kitchen a store-room, pantry and service porch.

There are four sleeping-rooms, all provided with good closet space, a bathroom and linen closet on the second floor; and on the third floor a billiard room or additional chamber, a servants' room,

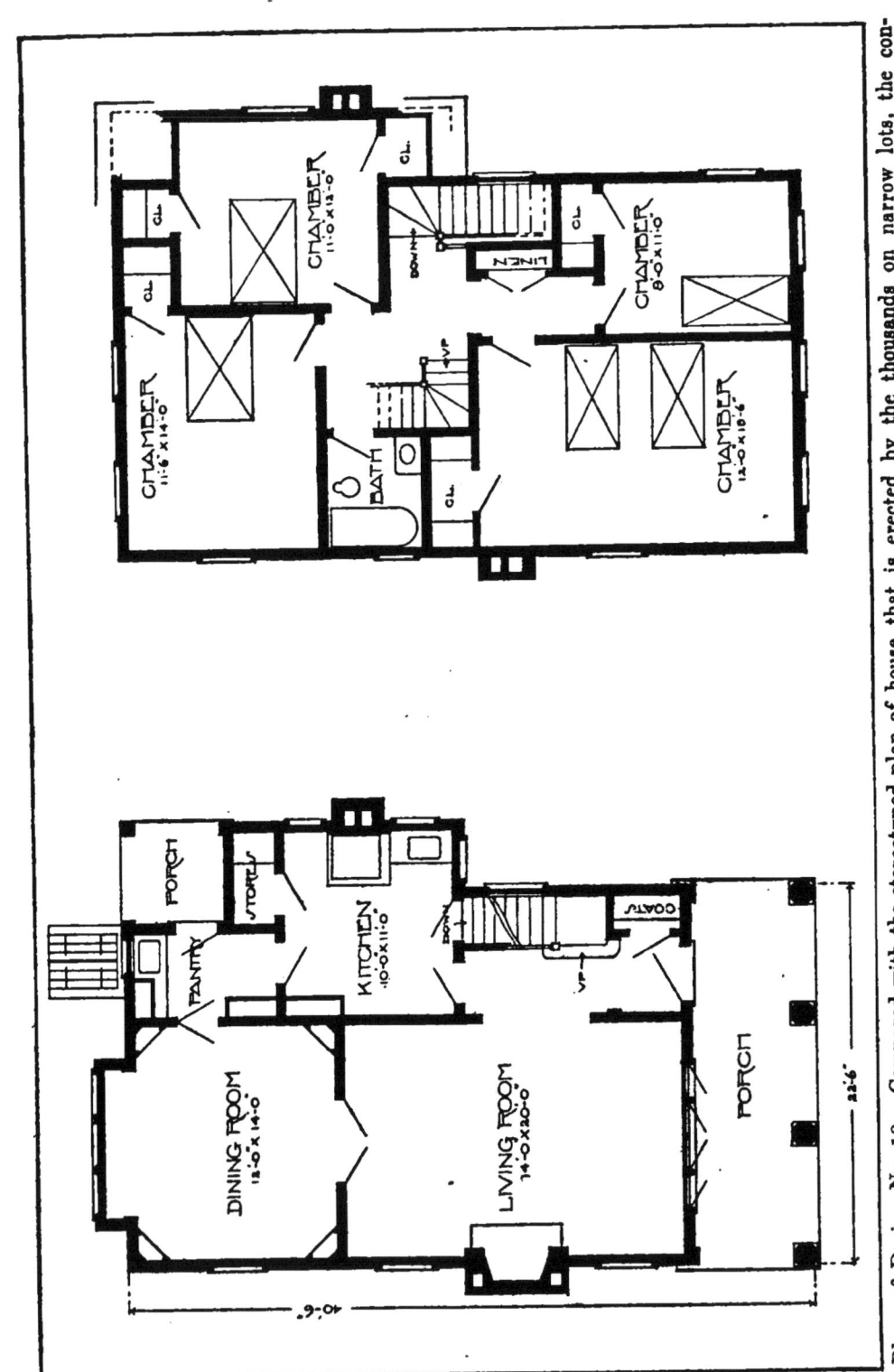

Plans of Design No. 10. Compared with the stereotyped plan of house that is erected by the thousands on narrow lots, the convenience and better appearance inside of this house must be evident.

Front and side elevations of Design No. 10. Shingles or clapboards might be substituted for the stucco walls, resulting, in most localities, in a saving in the cost

A STUCCO HOUSE

store-room and space for a bath if desired. The cellar contains the usual provision for heating plant, coal bins, servants' toilet, laundry with two tubs, and store-room.

In all probability this house will be built as one of a row on a comparatively narrow lot. A simple color scheme is suggested in order that the house may preserve its own dignity regardless of surrounding conditions. The stucco may be either white, gray or brownish yellow. The woodwork in each case should be white and the shingle roof moss green, deep rich red, or naturally weathered. The interior should be treated with a very simple trim, Colonial in character, and the walls be either papered or finished in rough plaster stained a warm gray, with white ceiling, or they may be light brown a trifle darker than the ceiling, which should be the same color.

The lawn in front of the house should have but little shrubbery, the garden effects being confined to the boundary lines. The paths may be of red brick, and a lattice archway, flanked on either side by well kept hedges running parallel with the street, will form a very pleasing entrance treatment.

The plan covers a ground area of 967 square feet and occupies approximately 29,977 cubic feet of space. The estimated cost is $4400 to $4800.

A HOUSE BASED ON THE NEW ENGLAND COLONIAL

DESIGN NO. 11

THE chief characteristics of New England Colonial architecture are the simplicity and beauty of its detail. In this example the points of interest are the wide clapboards, exposed ten inches to the weather, the recessed porches, and the pilaster treatment at the corners and at either side of the front porch. The perfect symmetry of the design produces a very restful and pleasing effect and suggests a home of refinement and culture. On the first floor a square entrance hall forms the central feature, which, simply and tastefully furnished, will produce a very agreeable impression when one first enters. A coat closet is concealed beneath the stairs. This hall separates the living-room from the dining-room and service quarters. In the dining-room are two quaint corner china-cupboards, suggestive of the period the house is intended to represent. Adjoining the kitchen are a service porch and store-room. On the second floor are four corner chambers, good closet room, bath and linen closet. In the attic there is space for a servants' room and store-room. The cellar provides for the customary laundry with stationary tubs, a servants' toilet, store-room for vegetables, etc., and a heater with two coal compartments.

In building a Colonial house of moderate cost where it is the owner's ambition to have his home executed in thorough harmony, it is well to remember that—especially in the environs of New York, where many fine old examples are constantly being demolished—it is not difficult to obtain fine specimens of mantels, doors and even staircase balustrades from house wreckers who carefully preserve for sale the best examples that come into their possession. It often hap-

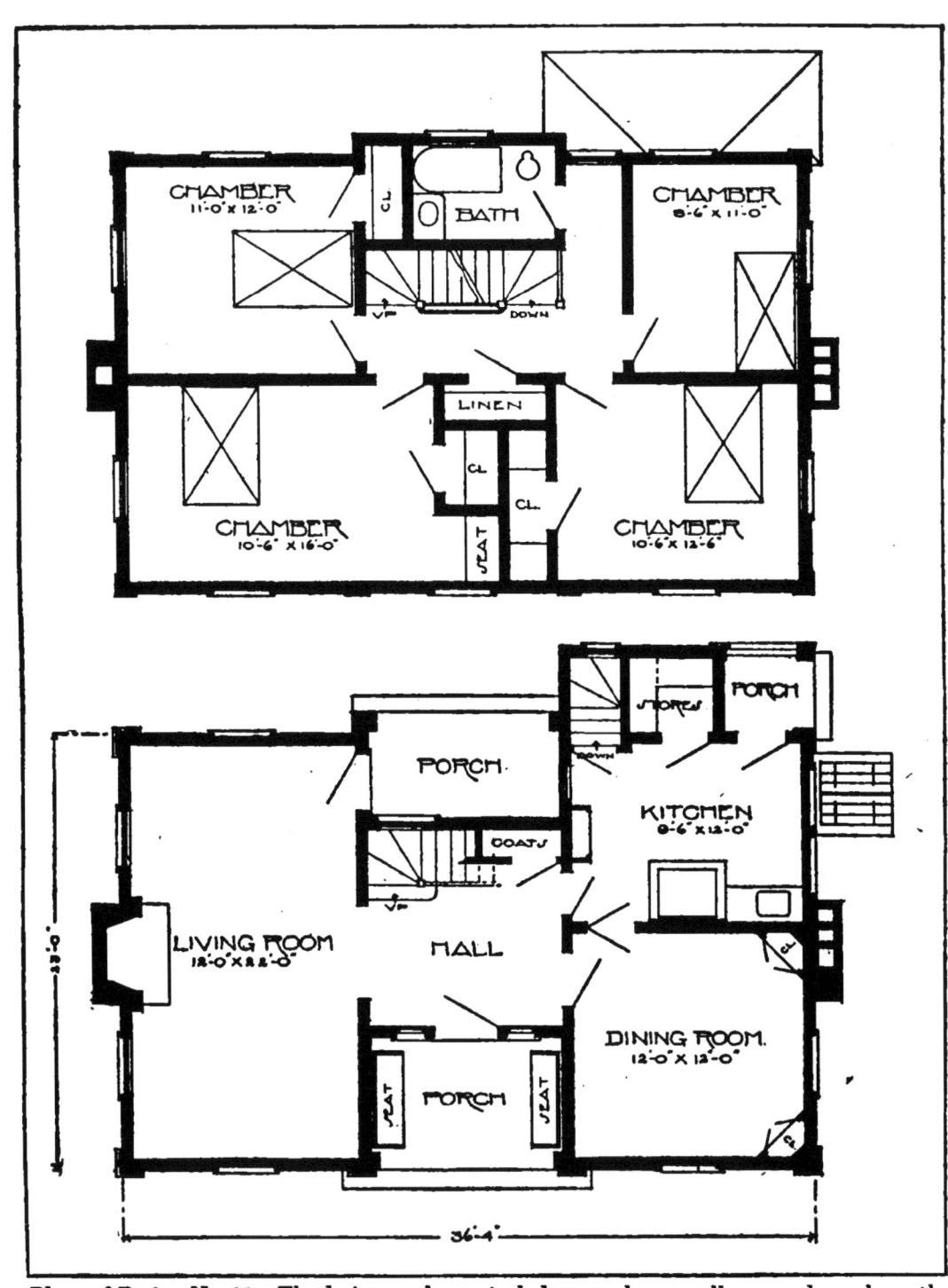

Plans of Design No. 11. The design as shown includes merely a small recessed porch on the front and a smaller one back of the hall. It would be an easy matter, if the site permitted, to add a porch across the whole fireplace side of the living-room.

Perspective view of Design No. 11. To many people no type has half the appeal of the stately New England Colonial with its delicately worked cornice and simple lines

NEW ENGLAND COLONIAL

pens that the most attractive features of a new Colonial house are the result of either having fragments from old houses installed, or the details of old work carefully followed in the new. It is optional with the owner, of course, whether or no he shall make the necessary effort to procure these details, which may easily add an historic interest to his home.

The exterior of this house should be white, with either white, gray or green blinds and exterior trim—in any case the sash and sashbars should be white. The roof should be of weathered shingles. The general interior treatment as to color should be the same as in house No. 8.

The house should face as nearly south as possible, veering towards the east if necessary. The planting should be more or less formal, box hedges and a rose garden perhaps forming important features.

This plan covers a ground area of 826 square feet, and occupies approximately 23,184 cubic feet of space. The estimated cost is $4000 to $4200.

A GABLED HOUSE OF HALF-TIMBER

DESIGN NO. 12

OWING to the increasing popularity of the English half-timbered house among home-builders in this country, the erection of the house herein described and illustrated will doubtless create favorable comment in any community. The striking exterior composition, as well as the admirable little plan, carefully studied and compactly arranged, will surely appeal to people of discernment and good taste. On the first floor a central hall separates the living-room from the dining-room. These two rooms, arranged on axis, create a pleasing vista and produce an effect suggesting greater space than really exists. A large corner porch, designed to receive the benefit of a summer breeze that may blow from almost any direction, is approached from two sides of the living-room. It does not, however, interfere with the direct lighting of this room, as there are windows both on the front and rear that are not darkened by the porch roof. The porch, enclosed in glass in winter, will make a most attractive sun parlor. A butler's pantry, porch and store-room in connection with the kitchen form the service equipment. On the second floor are three good-sized sleeping-rooms, having corner exposures, and a smaller fourth room which may be used either as a sleeping-room or sewing-room. On the third floor will be found accommodations for servants and a store-room. The cellar provides for a laundry with stationary tubs, servants' toilet, store-room for vegetables, etc., and a heater with two coal compartments.

The possibilities for elaboration in this home are more than usually great. The main rooms on the first floor, as well as the entrance hall and staircase hall, are most suitable for architectural treatment.

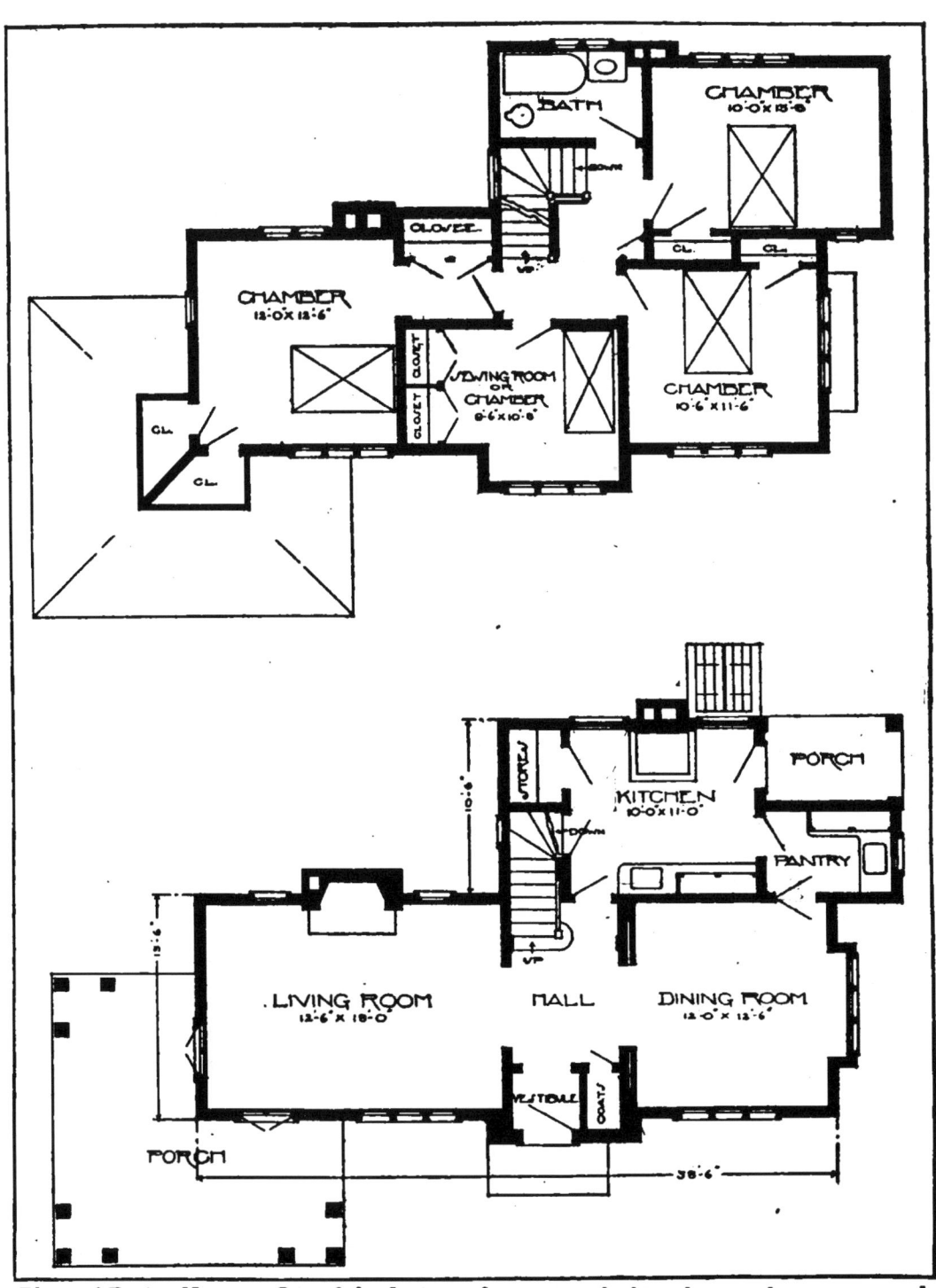

Plans of Design No. 12. One of the distinct advantages of this plan is the corner porch, which insures a breeze if there is one to be had. Incidentally, this location of porch gives opportunity for a very pleasing factor in the exterior appearance.

Perspective view of Design No. 12. Here too the half-timbering has been kept very simple in its design and quiet in tone. The leaded glass windows form an important element in the design

A GABLED HOUSE

Natural wood, wainscoted walls and beamed or ornamental plaster ceiling would be very appropriate. Although the house is quite complete without these additional features, it frequently happens that the owner wishes to improve his house each year and these suggestions apply in the case of the man who wishes to spend certain sums of money from time to time in decoration.

The porches should be floored with brick, quarry tile or cement. The brick flooring is extremely effective and is less expensive than tile. It would be advisable to use leaded glass for windows and doors throughout, in which case the sash should be painted lead color and all other exterior woodwork dark brown, except the roof, which should be weathered shingles. The half-timber work should be adzed to give the effect of hewn timbers. The stucco should be gray— different shades being applied to a small section of the house experimentally until the owner is satisfied with the result.

The house may face south or southeast. Expansive lawns with occasional groups of shrubbery, a formal garden and brick walls will form a pleasing setting for this house.

The plan covers a ground area of 791 square feet and occupies approximately 28,000 cubic feet of space. The cost is estimated at from $5000 to $5500.

A LONG GAMBREL-ROOF HOUSE

DESIGN NO. 18

THE long shallow plan of this gambrel-roofed cottage, accentuated at either end by porches, gives the effect from the front of a much larger house than it really is. A roomy hall separates the living-room from the dining-room and is also in communication with the kitchen, through a passageway from which lead the stairs to the cellar. The living-room opens upon a porch, indicated on the plan as being enclosed in glass. A similar porch extends beyond the dining-room and is shown open, though this arrangement may be reversed at the discretion of the prospective owner. The latter porch would make an excellent outdoor dining-room. Both porches are of the pergola type and both are roofed. A shingled hood, supported on brackets in front of the main entrance, produces a very pleasing feature and also serves as a protection in bad weather. In connection with the kitchen will be found a pantry, store-room and service porch. On the second floor are three sleeping-rooms, all with good closets, a bathroom and linen closet. In the attic ample space is provided for servants' room and store-room. In the cellar there is provision for a laundry with stationary tubs, servants' toilet, store-room for vegetables, etc., and a heater with the usual two coal compartments.

Shingles seem to be the most appropriate form of covering for the walls of this Dutch Colonial type. As in former designs, they look best when laid in broad courses. When shingles are to be white, an interesting effect is obtained by using a white shingle stain made to imitate the old Southern whitewash. This is taken care of in the specifications by an optional clause. The trim, brackets, col-

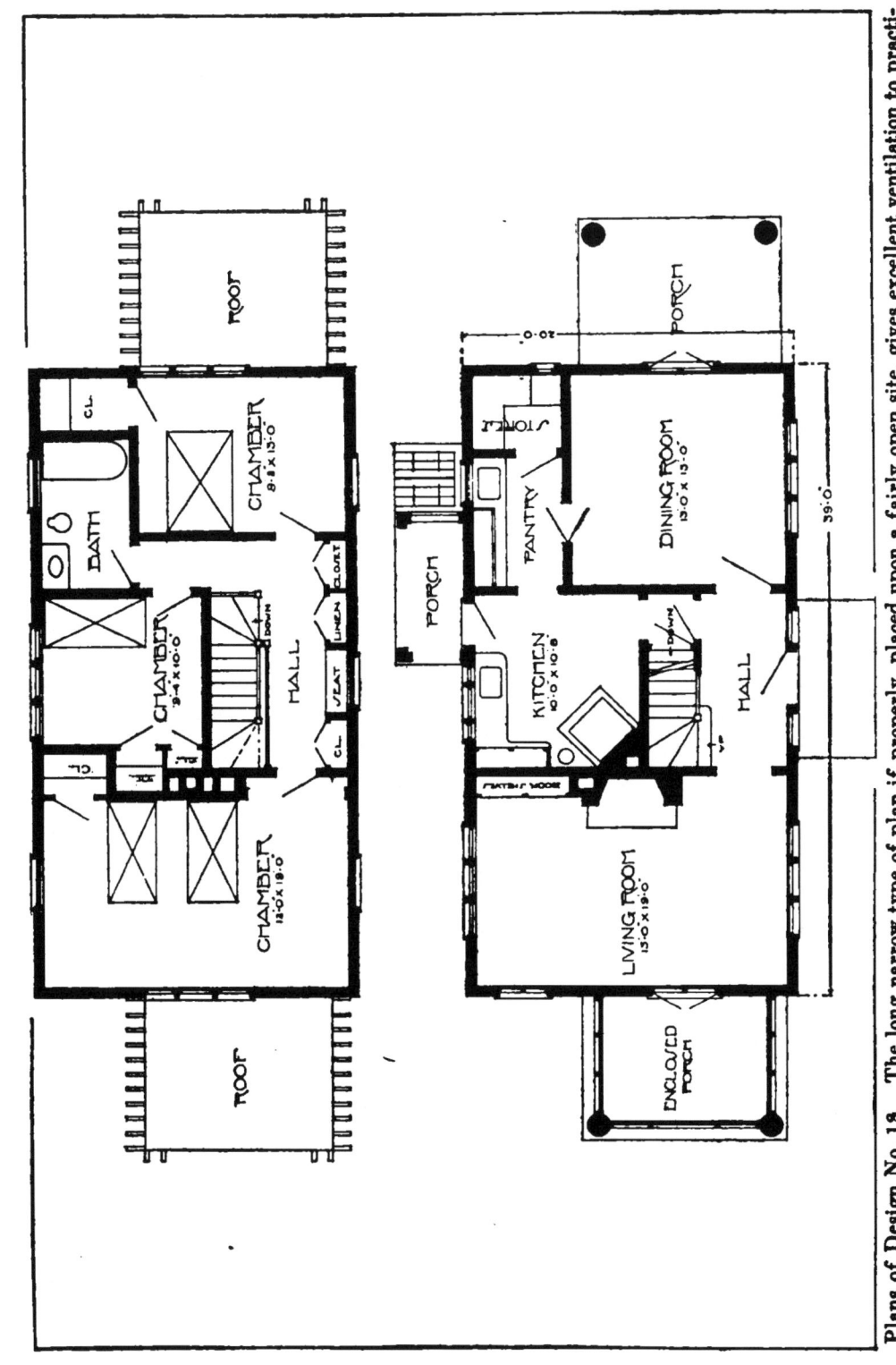

Plans of Design No. 18. The long narrow type of plan if properly placed upon a fairly open site, gives excellent ventilation to practically all the rooms.

Perspective view of Design No. 13. This gambrel-roof type with the continuous dormer windows has come to be a great favorite in the last few years, due to its possibilities for picturesque exterior appearence with an unexpectedly large amount of room upstairs

umns, rafters and sash should be white, with light green for the flower boxes and shutters. The roof may be stained a darker green or left to weather. We might say here that shingles weather much quicker on a roof than on side walls and in less than a year will turn gray.

As the living-room and dining-room are separated by the hall, these two rooms could have totally different color treatments. That is to say, one may be dark and the other light. Where the first floor hall is opened up into the second floor hall by a wide stair well, it is best to keep the color scheme the same for both.

If possible, face the house east or south. By so doing the principal rooms get the proper exposures for their respective uses.

The ground covered by this house is equal to 770 square feet and its contents approximately is 19,250 cubic feet. The cost will range from $3000 to $3200.

A SWISS CHALET
DESIGN NO. 14

FOR a summer house in the rugged mountainous regions or along the shores of almost any one of our beautiful American lakes, the Swiss châlet is without doubt the most pleasing and picturesque solution. The following illustrations will show what care has been devoted to the preperation of a design that embraces all of the salient features peculiar to the châlet without introducing the elaborate and costly details of the old examples, which in this age would cost fabulous sums to reproduce.

The arrangement of the first floor plan is well adapted for summer use. There are two porches, one running the entire depth of the house, and in direct communication with both living-room and dining-room; the other, a more formal entrance porch, opens from the living-room and entrance hall. The living-room and dining-room are connected by a wide opening which, at the discretion of the owner, may either have glazed doors or be without doors. The stairs to the second floor are open above the tread line on the living-room side, increasing the apparent size of this room as well as adding an interesting feature to the general treatment of the first floor interior scheme. There is a small room at the foot of the stairs that may be used as an office or den. The kitchen is provided with a store-room and service porch. The second floor contains four chambers, closets for each, a bath and linen closet and in the attic is space for servants' room and store-room. The cellar provides for a laundry with stationary tubs, servants' toilet, store-room for vegetables, etc., and a heater with two coal compartments.

To carry out the interior of this house in the most pleasing man-

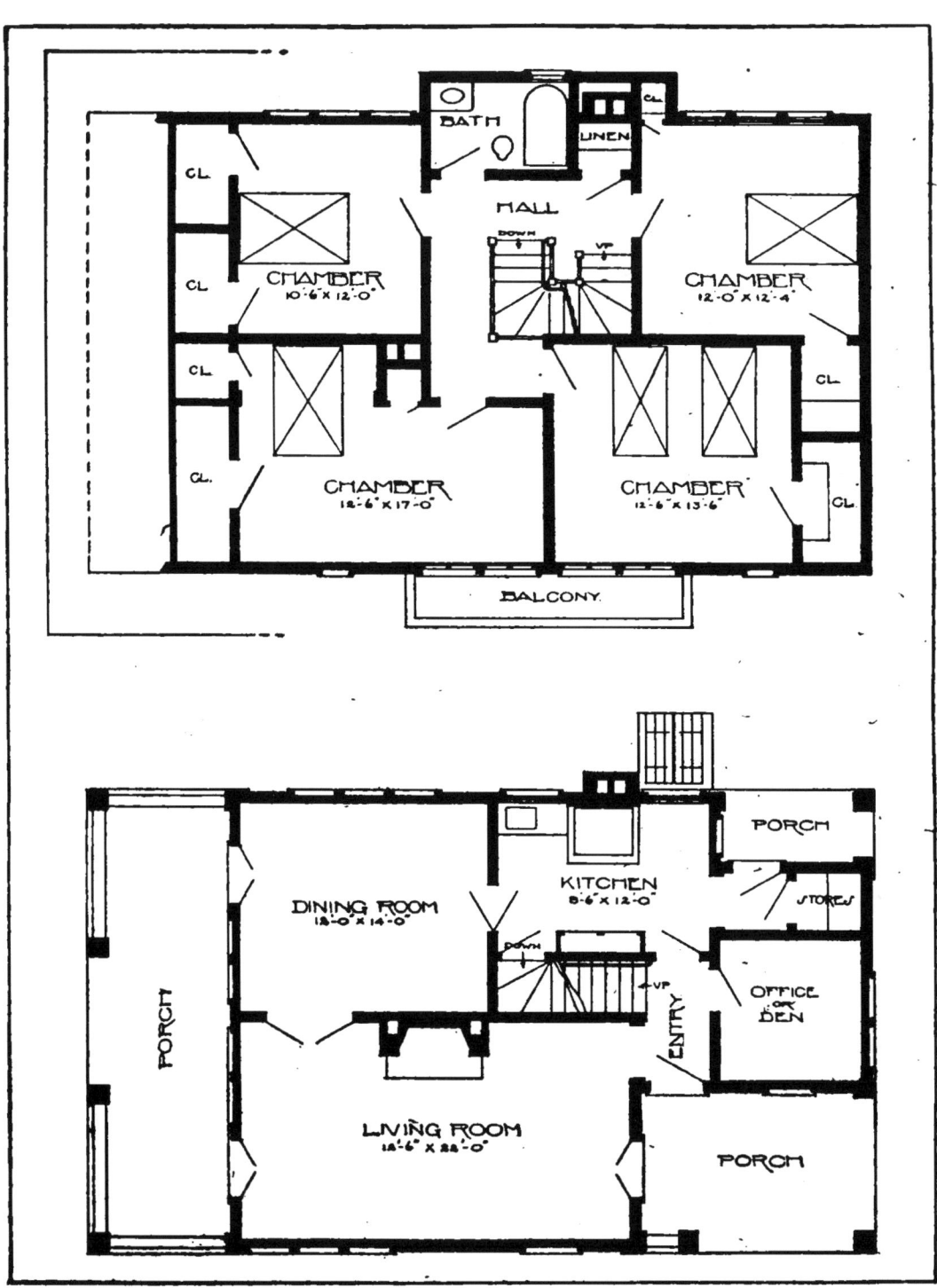

Plans of Design No. 14. The very nature of the Swiss châlet type requires a strictly rectangular plan without any excrescences on the first floor. The second-story closets are all built into the low slope of the roof.

Perspective view of Design No. 14. Upon the wonderful mountainsides of California the Swiss chalet type has been found to fit into the character of site as no other type possibly could. There are many opportunities for using the chalet type as a mountain home in the East as well

ner, it is necessary to depart from the more or less conventional treatment usually found in smaller homes. Rough plaster walls and plain wood trim may be used with excellent results, but there is an opportunity to add from time to time to this simple treatment, should the owner care to do so, by the installation of wainscotings and beamed ceilings, both of which would be most appropriate. The woodwork of the exterior may be stained a chestnut brown or a weathered gray, in which latter case a sand-blast finish applied to certain portions of the building would add greatly to the texture of the wood and produce an aged effect which would greatly enhance its beauty. Weathered shingles would produce the best effect on the roof.

The planting in the immediate vicinity of the house should be more or less rugged to harmonize with what in all probability will form the natural surroundings. The house may face northeast to advantage.

This plan covers a ground area of 986 square feet and occupies approximately 26,208 cubic feet of space. The estimated cost is $5500 to $6000.

A MODIFIED COLONIAL COTTAGE

DESIGN NO. 15

THE accompanying plans illustrate a distinctive summer cottage, very simple in outline, though possessing interesting features which render it extremely picturesque. As in house No. 1, the living-room and dining-room are combined, opening in front upon the covered porch through three French windows and at the sides upon small Dutch porches uncovered except for lattice arches. It is an open air house and intended for summer use. Aside from the living-room, dining-room and kitchen, one chamber and the bath are located on the first floor. The bath at the foot of the stairs is situated in a position to be convenient to the second floor chambers. It is located on the first floor because it frequently happens that the natural water supply in remote districts does not go above this floor. It would be quite possible to convert this house into an all-year house by certain minor changes. A partition could be run across the living-room at the end of the mantel on the pantry side, forming two separate rooms. A vestibule could be built where the Dutch porch occurs on the living-room end and a bath be installed on the second floor where the window-seat is shown at the head of the stairs. This would give a house with four chambers, three on the second floor and one on the first floor, all with cross ventilation and ample closet room; two bathrooms and a linen closet. If the bath on the second were installed, the one on the first could easily be omitted, throwing more space into the first floor chamber. The cellar provides for a laundry with stationary

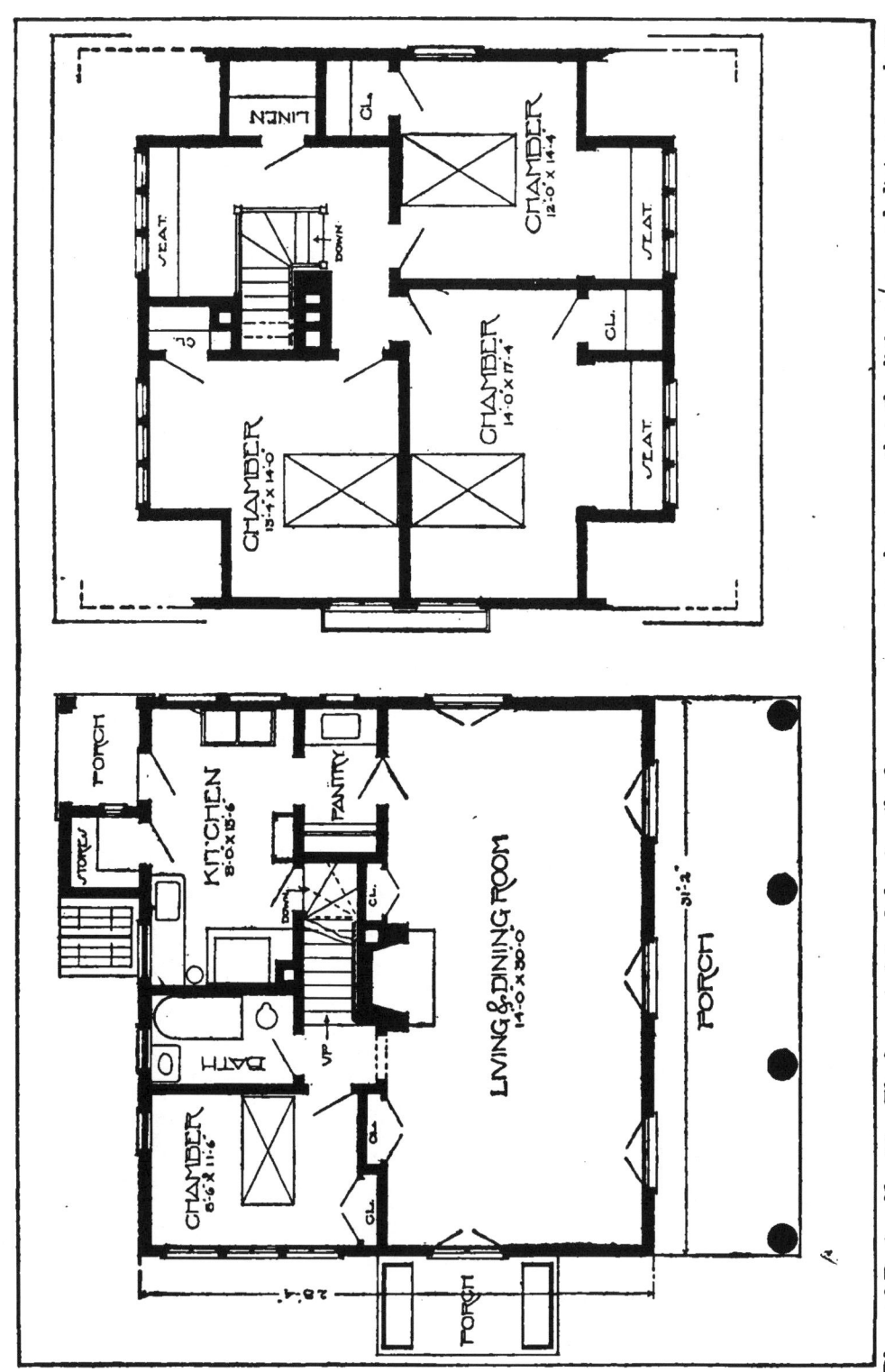

Plans of Design No. 15. The house is intended primarily for use as a summer home, so that the living-room and dining-room have been combined to give a very large room

Perspective view of Design No. 15. Here is another design intended mainly for use as a summer home, although with certain changes indoors it could be readily used throughout the year

111

A COLONIAL COTTAGE

tubs, servants' toilet, store-room for vegetables, etc., and a heater with two coal compartments.

If the sides are of shingles and the situation is inclined to be rugged, then allow the shingles to weather and tone in with surrounding Nature. With the ordinary white cedar shingle this takes some time, often as long as two years. In this case a gray stain may be used. If the side walls are of clapboards or siding, then white paint is best. In either case keep all the sash and trim white. If the body is white, then green in some light tone would be pleasing for the lattice, seats and flower box.

For the average summer home, the first floor in dark wood is both durable and attractive. The bedrooms, however, are best in white and in this house, with simple chintz curtains at the windows, they would be cozy and inviting.

Here again, by facing the long side of the living-room east or south, the sun and breeze are obtained at the right hours.

The ground area is 930 square feet and the contents 24,180 cubic feet. The cost will run from $3500 to $3800.

A SMALL DUTCH COLONIAL HOUSE

DESIGN NO. 16

A VERY interesting example of Dutch Colonial has been evolved in the creating of this house. It will be seen from the photographs on the pages following that unlimited care has been devoted to its composition, and although it is one of the smallest and least expensive to construct among this entire collection, it still possesses individual characteristics which enable it to appear to advantage in any community. The house is intended for occupancy during the entire year. It will be seen that the first floor plan is very compact. The entrance hall has been omitted in order to give greater space in the living quarters. In winter the seats on the entrance porch may be removed and a storm door erected as a protection against draughts in the living-room when the door is opened.

The interior treatment of this house is quite as interesting as the exterior, and altogether it may be considered a success from the standpoint of small house architecture. There are three chambers on the second floor, all having cross ventilation and good closet room, also a bath and linen closet combined. The cellar provides for a laundry with stationary tubs, servants' toilet, store-room for vegetables, etc., and a heater with two coal compartments.

To refer to the floor plans again, notice should be given to the utility of every inch of available space. While the kitchen is small, it will be found a very convenient working room and a great step-saver. By having a table tucked in under the porch window, the housewife may stand in the center of the room and with one step,

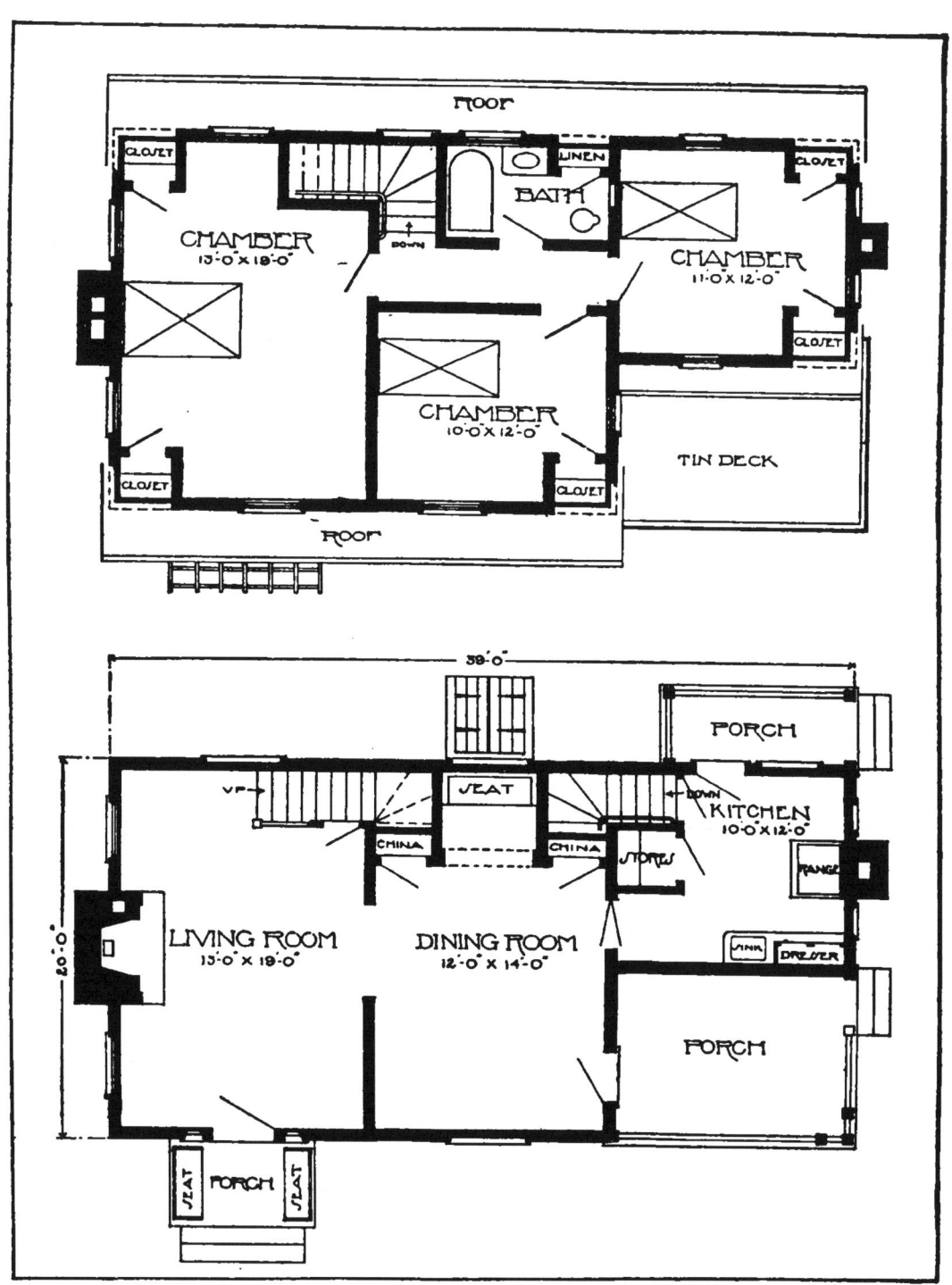

Plans of Design No. 16. Another interesting variation of the long narrow plan. If one does not mind having the front door open directly into the living-room, much space can be saved that would otherwise be needed for a hall.

Design No. 16, from a photograph. The entrance doorway opens directly into the living-room. In winter the seats might be removed and a vestibule built in their place as a protection against drafts

DUTCH COLONIAL HOUSE

reach the range, sink, closet and the doors to the dining-room and to the cellar.

The house, as built and shown in the photographs, has widely spaced shingles. The walls are stained a silvery gray and all trim and other exterior woodwork are white, except the shutters and flower boxes which are green. The roof has been left to weather a gray, darker than the walls. This style of house would look equally as well in white for all parts except the shutters and flower boxes, which should remain green. The location has something to do with the color scheme. If set in a wealth of trees, all white gives a cool and restful air.

The interior of this house has been treated in white except the dining-room, which is in natural finish chestnut, and the kitchen, which is painted a warm gray. The floors are hard pine rubbed down to a wax finish.

By facing the house either south or east good exposures are obtained. Here again a reversal of the plan may give better results.

The ground area covered is 668 square feet and the cubical contents approximately 18,904 cubic feet. The cost in most sections would be from $3000 to $3500.

The house as built has widely spaced shingles stained silvery grey, with the outside woodwork white, excepting the second-story shutters which are green

Design No. 16, from a photograph. It will be seen that the rear of the house is scarcely less attractive than the front. In the background may be seen the rear of Design No. 19

AN INFORMAL ENGLISH COTTAGE

DESIGN NO. 17

THE drawings show a very charming little house, possessing many of the characteristics of the English stucco cottage. The graceful lines and long sloping roof form a picturesque composition of great merit. One of the many advantages of this plan is the fact that it is admirably suited to a small lot, in which case the porch gable will face the street. If, on the other hand, the dimensions of the property permit, the long front may face the street with an effect equally pleasing.

The entrance door opens from the spacious porch into a compact hall, from which may be entered through separated doors the living-room, dining-room and kitchen. From the left of this hall the stairs lead to the second floor and under the stairs is a roomy coat closet. The arrangement of dining-room and living-room have a tendency to exaggerate their actual size. The kitchen, which opens directly into the dining-room, possesses a large store-closet and service porch. On the second floor are four sleeping-rooms, a good closet for each one, a linen closet and bath. Three of the sleeping-rooms are corner rooms. The cellar provides for a laundry with stationary tubs, servants' toilet, a store-room for vegetables, etc., and a heater with two coal compartments. The cellar floor is of concrete and in front of the tubs a movable slat platform is placed. This gives a comfortable footing and at the same time allows the floor to be washed and scrubbed with the minimum effort. We all know how dirt collects in the cellar when the floor is of wood.

The charm of stucco lies not so much in its color or in its appearance of solid masonry, as in its texture. The variety of surfaces

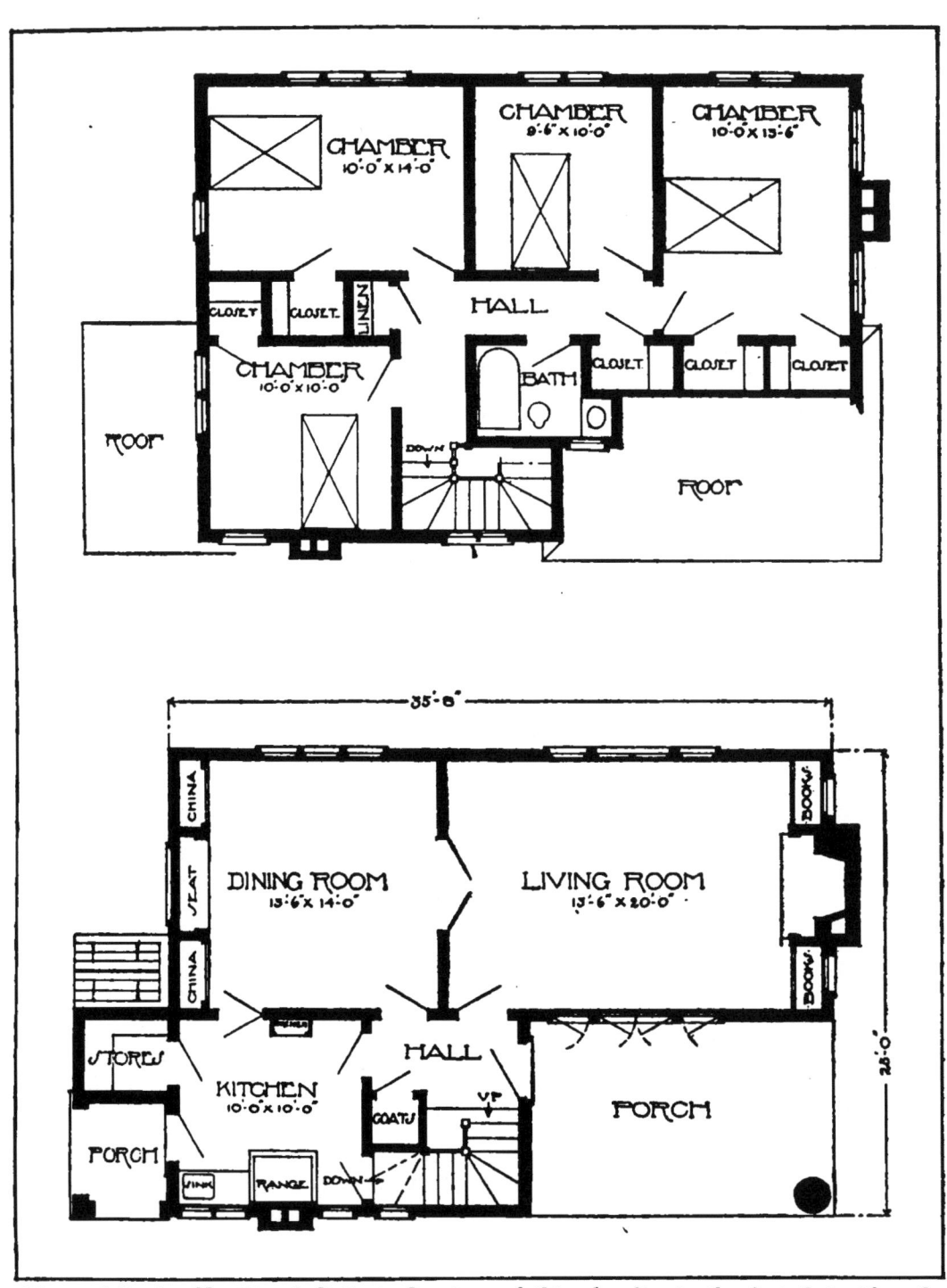

Plans of Design No. 17. A distinct advantage of this plan lies in the fact that either the long porch side or the chimney end may face the street, making it available for use on a narrow lot.

Perspective view of Design No. 17. Another adaptation of the English cottage type in stucco. A moderately rough-textured wall in a light grey or cream, with a grey shingled roof, would be a pleasing combination

INFORMAL ENGLISH COTTAGE

is almost endless. From a smooth troweled finish up to the roughest of rough-cast, we have a choice to fit every type of stucco house. Naturally, the more formal treatments require a smoother wall than the treatments where picturesqueness and broadness are sought after.

For this house we suggest a moderately rough surface. While the house is not of sufficient size to admit of very broad wall areas without openings, yet the general treatment is informal and a smooth finish would be out of place.

The color of the stucco should be light. The dark slaty or mud color so often seen would entirely spoil the effect of this house and destroy the values of the plain wall surfaces. We advise either a light gray or a cream color, for then, by treating the woodwork in white, a subtle contrast is obtained. This is more endurable than strong, sharp notes which soon lose their pristine effect and become displeasing to one obliged constantly to see the house.

If the stucco has a decided color tone, such as cream, a gray roof is best. This gray may be obtained by letting the shingles weather or by using a stain. However, if the stucco turns out a light gray, then a red or green roof is possible.

This house has 728 square feet of ground area and approximately 18,075 cubic feet. The cost is from $3600 to $3800.

A FRAME HOUSE OF ITALIAN SIMPLICITY

DESIGN NO. 18

THIS frame house possesses the simple Italian feeling which, aside from producing a particularly pleasing effect, is a most economical type to construct. The little entrance porch, with the flower box above, is a very attractive feature, setting off the rather severe lines of the house to great advantage. The main entrance leads into a small hall or vestibule, on the left of which is the living-room and on the right the dining-room, both bright, well proportioned rooms. A coat closet is placed under the main stairs, which lead up both from the living-room and the kitchen, a very desirable feature in a small house where there is no staircase hall. A spacious porch extends the entire depth of the house, adjoining the living-room. A good-sized store-room and service porch are provided in connection with the kitchen. On the second floor are three sleeping-rooms, all provided with closets and all having cross ventilation. There is also a bath and a linen closet. In the cellar there is a laundry with stationary tubs, a servants' toilet, store-room for vegetables, etc., and a heater with compartments for its own coal and that for the kitchen range.

It is an important element in the success of this design that the windows are divided into lights as shown. With this division a richness is effected that would be entirely lost if they were omitted. In this latter case the appearance of the exterior would be of bareness and poverty.

Both shingles and clapboards will look well on this house. Here is another instance where white seems to be the most appropriate color, whether shingles or clapboards are used. The house, being

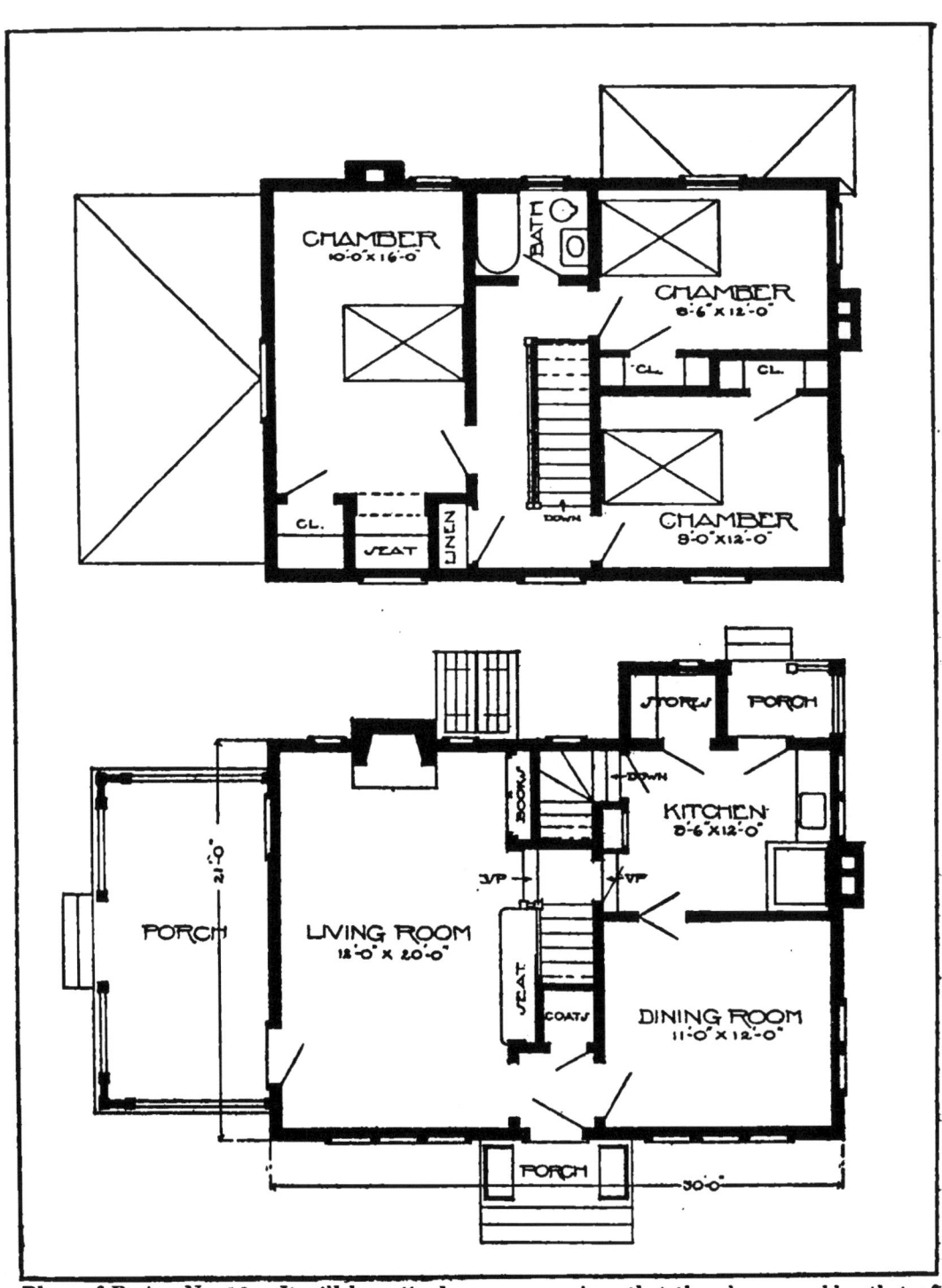

Plans of Design No. 18. It will be noticed upon comparison that the plan resembles that of Design No. 8, particularly on the first floor, but it is somewhat smaller.

Perspective view of Design No. 18. Either shingles or clapboards would look well upon the walls, but in either case white will be the most appropriate color. White always increases the apparent size of a building

one of the smallest shown, would look very insignificant if treated with a dark color. White, on the contrary, always increases the apparent size of a building and gives it a certain dignified appearance, hardly obtainable with any other color.

A red-stained roof will give the needed color and with foliage well placed about it, a delightful combination is possible.

One color scheme for both dining-room and living-rooms would be simple and restful. This is in keeping with a small house, where too many motifs or color schemes are out of place.

The house may face either east or south for the best exposures.

The plan covers in ground area 630 square feet and occupies approximately 17,640 cubic feet of space. The cost will run from $2800 to $3000.

A COLONIAL HOUSE OF SIMPLE LINES

DESIGN NO. 19

THE design gives an example of early Colonial architecture possessing the many charming and homelike characteristics peculiar to this style. The long lines of the gambrel roof give the appearance of a low rambling house and offset the stilted effect so often seen in two-story houses of the smaller variety. The interior of this house is surprisingly commodious. On the first floor will be found a large living-room, connected with the dining-room by an arched passage the depth of the fireplace, a good-sized porch and sun parlor, all of which are connected by means of French windows, giving a very spacious appearance to the living quarters. This sun parlor may well be omitted if a larger living-porch is desired. In this case the porch should take up the exact amount of space now occupied by the sun parlor. The kitchen, which communicates directly with the entrance hall, is provided with a large storeroom and service porch. In this plan there is also a space allotted to the wash-tubs, though accommodations for a laundry in the cellar are provided for. The second floor contains four corner chambers with generous closet space, a bath and linen closet. A staircase leads to the attic, in which there is sufficient space for a small servants' room. The cellar provides for a laundry with stationary tubs, servants' toilet, store-room for vegetables, etc., and a heater with two coal compartments.

There is but one color, white, for the body of this house. With this we secure a very delicate contrast by painting the lattice, flower box and shutters a light green. The lattice helps wonderfully in carrying out the horizontal effect aimed at in designing this house.

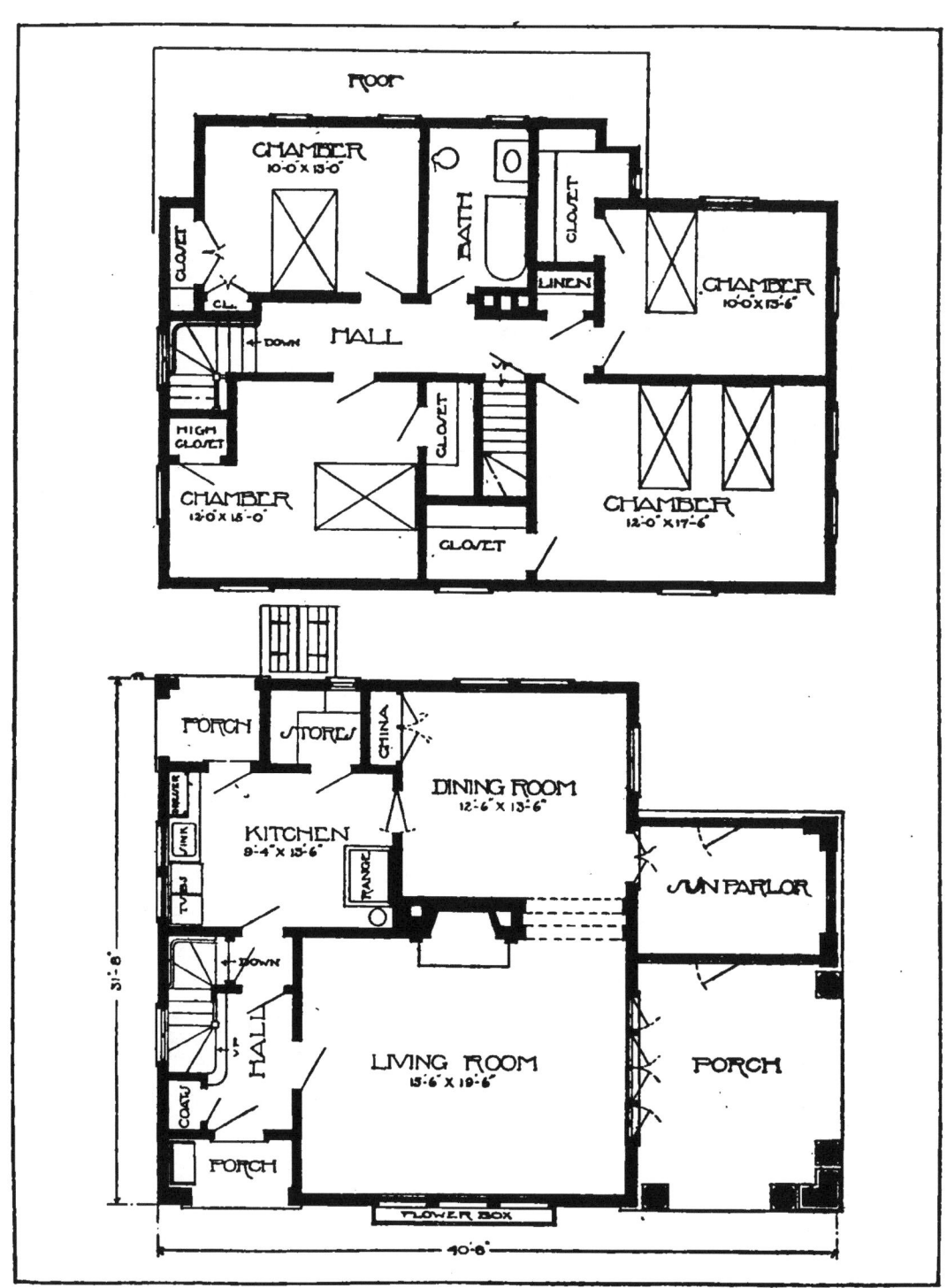

Plans of Design No. 19. To those who would like to depart widely from the stereotyped exterior, while adhering closely to an attractive simplicity, this house will have a strong appeal. There is an unusually large amount of space in the second floor.

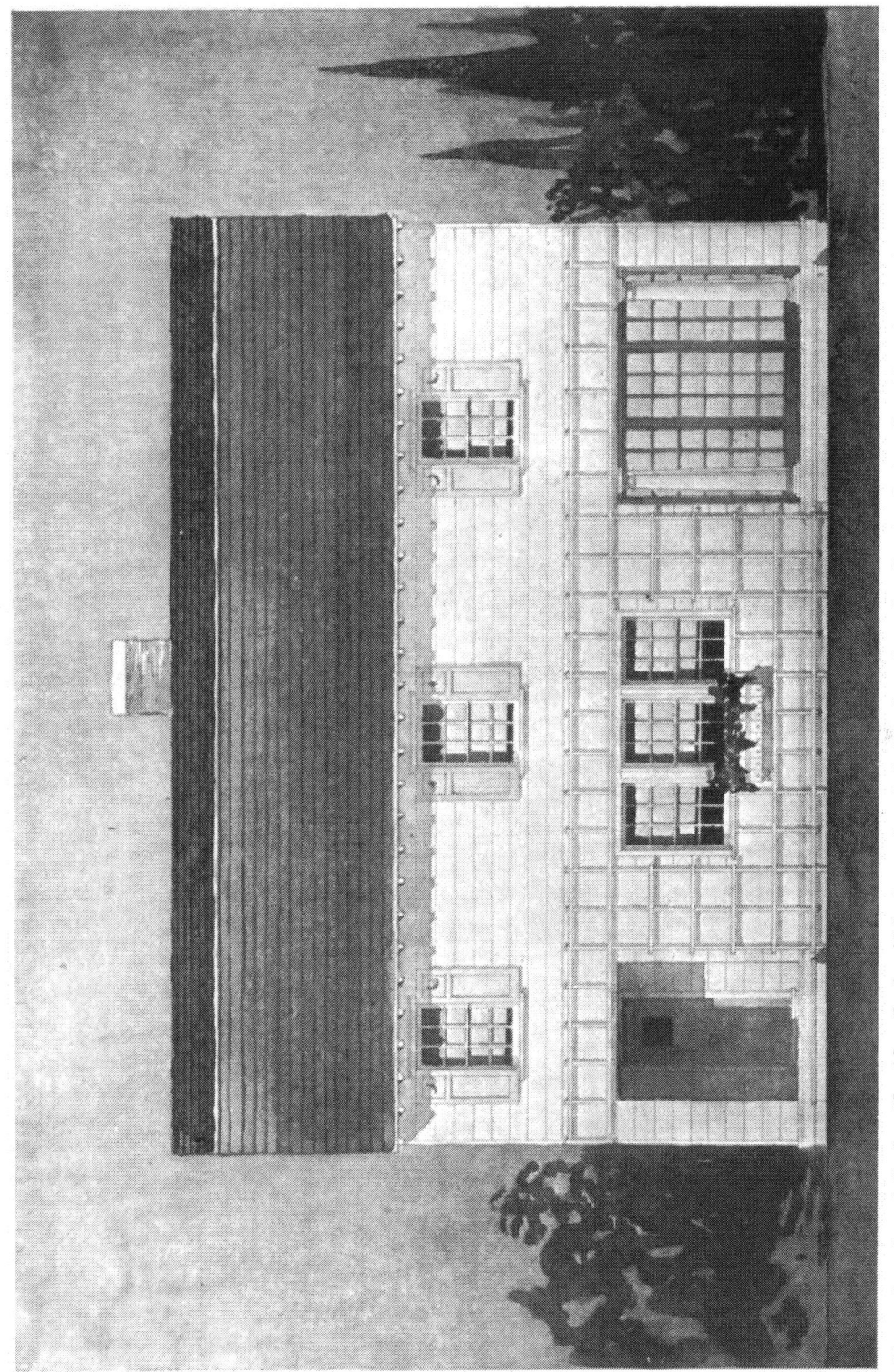

Front elevation of Design No. 19. It should be borne in mind that the minor details of a design like this—the specially designed shutters, the latticework and flower box—are of the utmost importance in giving the house a certain note of distinction

Imagine the lattice covered with a crimson rambler vine in blossom and backed by the white walls and trim!

Here the windows should be divided into lights as shown. Each one is placed for a spot of decoration with a restful wall space between and therefore they should have as much sparkle and interest as possible. Keep every part of these windows white except the blinds, which are light green as described above.

Lose no time, after completing this house, in planting the vines for the latticework, as much of the final effect of the house depends upon them.

Face the front of the house west. This will bring the sun into the dining-room during the morning and in the sun parlor all day long. The next best position would be facing south, but this is not as advantageous as the other.

With this type of house, a bit of formal gardening goes well. Some of the old-fashioned flowers arranged along graveled walks with arbors and trellises, would be quite in spirit with the style.

The area covered by this house is 1188 square feet and it contains approximately 33,124 cubic feet. However, on account of its simple structural lines, the cost is from $4500 to $5000.

A COMBINATION OF STUCCO WITH HALF-TIMBER GABLES

DESIGN NO. 20

IN this house the main walls are of stucco with half-timbered gables and brick chimneys. The general effect is rather imposing and, notwithstanding the moderate sum for which this house can be erected, it will create a favorable impression in a community where the average home is far more costly and pretentious. In the main this house is more adaptable to a site possessing a pleasing outlook in all directions with possibilities for garden and formal landscape treatment, though very pleasing effects may always be obtained on a small lot.

In the plan of the house it will be seen that the living-porches, two in number, have been kept apart from the main entrance, thus permitting a greater degree of seclusion for the members of the family. The size of the porch at the left is optional with the owner and is only limited in the design in order that the completed house may come within the estimated cost. The entrance hall opens directly into the dining-room and living-room and through a passage into the kitchen. The dining-room and living-room are connected, and from the living-room a very pleasing view of the tile-paved bay in the dining-room may be obtained. This bay is intended as a small conservatory, in which capacity it would prove most effective, as it is visible from both the main living-rooms as well as from the hall. On the second floor are four sleeping-rooms with ample closet room, linen closet and bath. Each of the bedrooms is a corner room. The cellar provides for a laundry with stationary tubs, servants' toilet, a store-room for vegetables, etc., and a heater with two coal compartments.

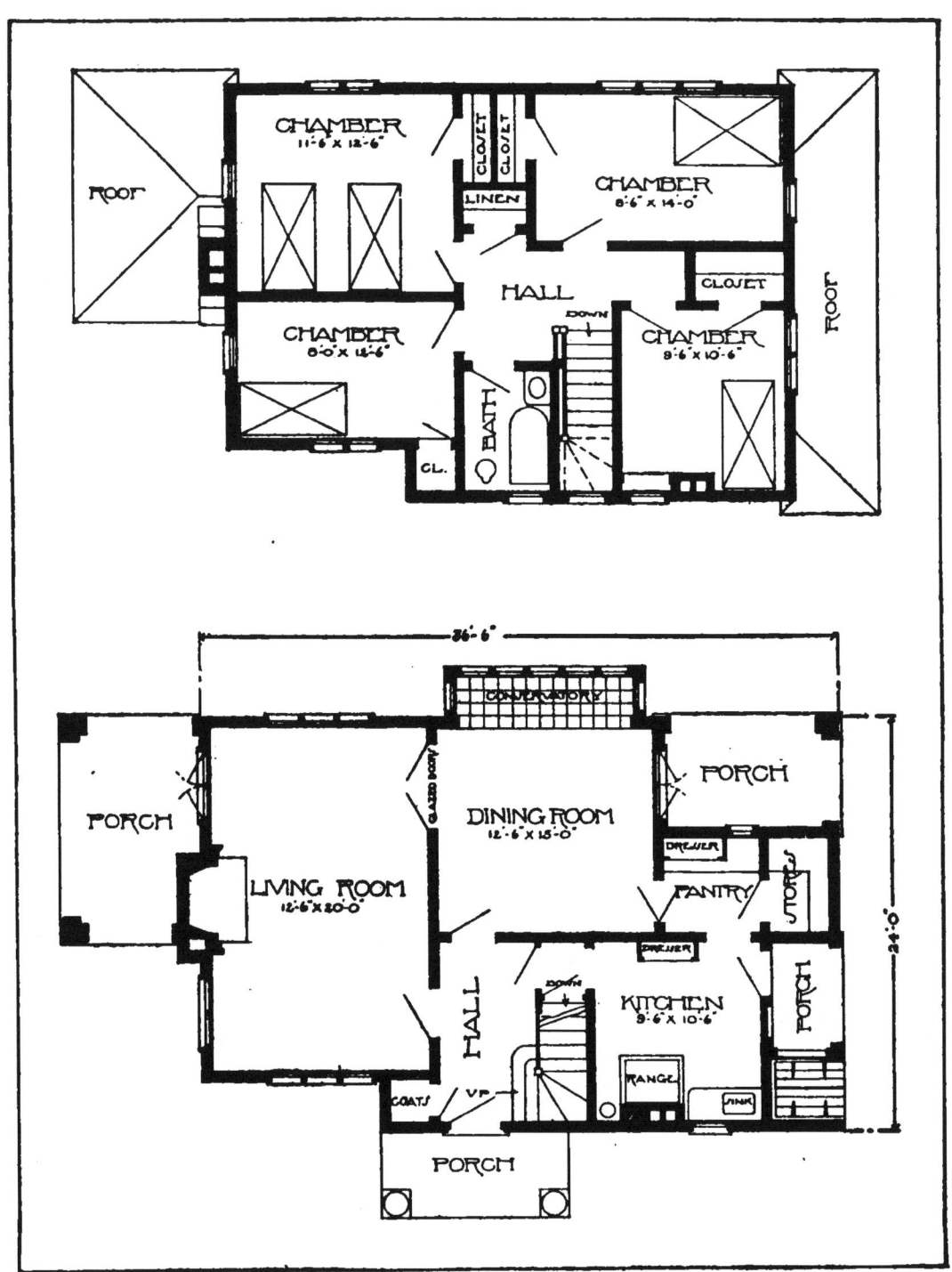

Plans of Design No. 20. A noteworthy advantage of this plan lies in the two porches, both of which are so located that they may be used with a large degree of privacy.

Perspective view of Design No. 20. The materials that have been used in this design—brick, stucco and half-timber—give it an air of permanence that these more substantial materials always bring

A COMBINATION OF STUCCO

The stucco on the walls of this house may be a bit smoother than the walls described for the design shown as No. 17. Here the stucco comes in connection with half-timber work. Besides, the design is somewhat more formal and imposing as will be evident from the drawings. Here also the color should be light, for with our red brick and brown timberwork we need enough contrast to set off these other two materials. If the stucco is dark, the vertical lines in the gable ends lose their effect entirely. To avoid too strong contrast, all exterior wood should be a warm brown, even the sash. The introduction of white would give too sharp a note.

To place this house to the best advantage as to exposure, the long side of the living-room should face east. This will give a southern exposure for one side and a chance for the sun to reach the dining-room during the morning.

The square feet of ground covered is 748 and the cubical contents is approximately 20,944 cubic feet. The cost ranges from $4000 to $4500.

A STUCCO COTTAGE

DESIGN NO. 21

AN attractive stucco cottage is here presented, the plain, simple lines of which are admirably suited to economical construction. The steep sloping roof and pergola porch (which is roofed over) lend distinction to the design. This porch may be carried the entire width of the house, if so desired, by the addition of two columns and a very slight extra cost if the change is made before going ahead with the work.

The arrangement of the plans is the most economical possible. On the first floor a central entrance hall divides the living-room from the dining-room, an arrangement many people prefer to the type of house in which these two rooms are intercommunicating. A door leading directly from the kitchen and a landing on the stair renders communication between the service quarters and the second floor possible without going through the main living-rooms. The kitchen is provided with a store-room, pantry, porch and all the other necessary equipment. On the second floor will be found four chambers, each having cross ventilation and ample closet room, as well as a bath and linen closet combined. Excellent storage space is provided for in the attic. The cellar provides for a laundry with stationary tubs, servants' toilet, store-room for vegetables, etc., and a heater with two coal compartments.

If the stucco is light, treat the sash in a light brown and the other woodwork white. The rafter-ends of both the roof and porch would also look well in brown. In all cases keep the columns white. Columns that are any other color lose all the charm of their detail and proportion; they become dead, instead of being full of life, as a well designed column should be. Remember one thing: you can never

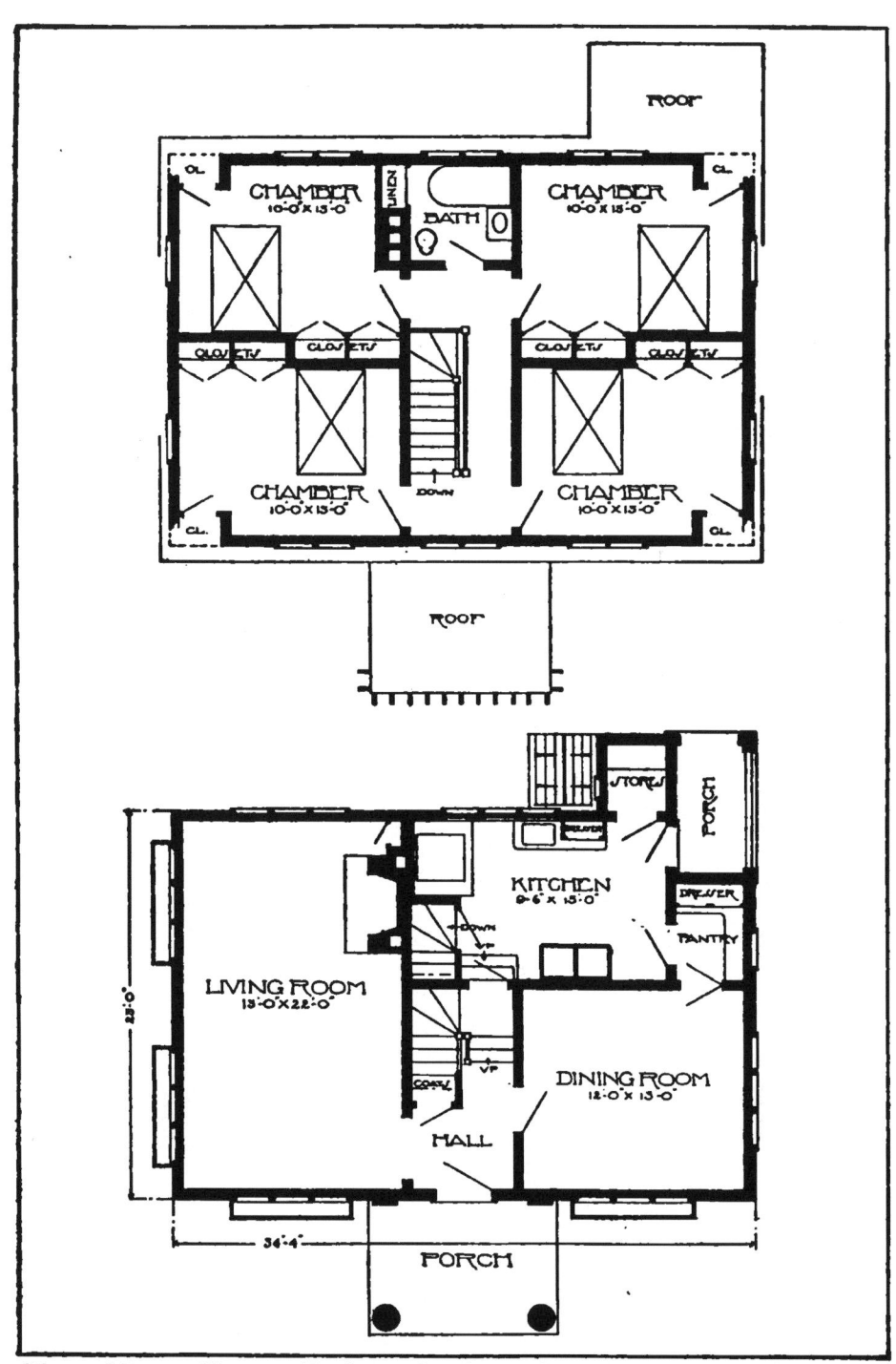

Plans of Design No. 21. To those who like windows in plenty—a fresh-air house throughout—this plan will offer an especial appeal. The windows, so far as possible, have been grouped, giving a pleasing appearance from both inside and out.

Perspective view of Design No. 21. The steep sloping roof, the long continuous dormers and the grouped windows are the chief elements in the design of this simple stucco cottage

make a mistake by painting all exterior woodwork of a stucco house, white. No matter what the color of the stucco, white will always tone in and produce a harmony, unless, of course, the stucco is a dark slate, and then the contrast is too strong by far. Red or green stain will go well on the roof.

A good treatment for the interior of this little cottage is to make all downstairs woodwork in a natural, rather dark finish and all upstairs white. In a small house a sudden change from a very light colored room to a very dark one is sometimes disquieting.

Face the house south or east and you have the proper exposures for sun and breeze.

In ground area the plan covers 782 square feet and has approximately 21,896 cubic feet for its contents, while the cost is from $3400 to $3600.

Printed in Great Britain
by Amazon